BEYROUTES
A Guide to Beirut

BEYROUTES
A Guide to Beirut

Initiated by Studio Beirut

TABLE OF CONTENT

EMOTIONAL CITY

INVENTED CITY

FOREWORD

The destination of this book is Beirut, a fabulous city on the Mediterranean. It is one of the grand capitals of the Middle East, a product of the most intricate and explosive historical cocktail imaginable.

Very few cities in the world are as fragmented and offer as many layers of meaning as Beirut. This guide consists of a variety of subjective explorations of the city's diversity and communality, its public and private spaces. It provides the reader with multiple perceptions of these layers via four ways of re-scripting Beirut - The First Impression City, The Official City, The Invented City, and The Emotional City - which shows the complexity of how one gets to know this city, its inhabitants, its buildings, and its everyday life. As such, Beyroutes offers a whole different set of 'rules of navigation' for the Lebanese metropolis at this particular moment of time.

This guide project and its preceding workshops were an initiative of the members of Studio Beirut, supported by Archis, Partizan Publik, and the Pearl Foundation. The contributors consist of a varied group of individuals: Beirutis from north, south, east, west and central parts of the city, old and young guys and girls from the Diaspora, foreigners who are long term residents, as well as frequent and first-time visitors. In the series of workshops, participants worked together, driven by a common fascination for exploring and understanding Beirut, and a desire to engage with it. As such *Beyroutes* is the result of many differing viewpoints and experiences of the city.

Archis has published *Beyroutes* as the first in a series of guides that take the human infrastructure of cities as a point of departure. Due to the generous support of the Prince Claus Fund, the Fund for the Quality of Living, the Netherlands Embassy in Lebanon and the Zico House, the authors of *Beyroutes* invite you to engage with Beirut and to give the city something in return of your experiences.

Christian Ernsten

8

Photo by Nicolas Bourquin

MY CITY

A guide book is funny in many ways. Funny because you start writing its introduction only when you're about to finish its content.

A normal guide to Beirut is even funnier because it starts with the hypothesis of having to follow certain patterns: it tells you about the nice weather, the great food and the friendly people (or not). It elusively mentions power but talks more in-depth about photography restrictions, the absurdities of standing in line, people staring and the Lebanese special driving skills. It will discuss the Lebanese blending of at least three languages, teach you to smoke arguileh or to dance dabkeh, inform you on the difference between taxis and the infamous service, and tell you that your food will be delivered on a faster track than the one that the police needs to help damsels in distress. It even advises you where to go out and especially when to visit.

There is however a discrepancy between projecting the image of a so-called normal and healthy city, and the image representing a city like Beirut. The capital of Lebanon has always been the land of the small but hard headed refugees who, throughout history, as minorities have sheltered in its mountains, with no conflict or understanding has ever lead to a common vision for all communities. We are told that wars do not determine who is right, only who is left. Imagine a scenario where everybody is left and there are no victors, everything becomes subject to interpretation, even historical events (Lebanon does not have a common history book to this day). No wonder that the limits between public and private in Beirut are superfluous, for if we take two steps back, Lebanon itself is a sort of regional public space. And as any public space should act, Lebanon, and especially its capital Beirut, is the stage of all types contradictions, eccentricities and passions.

All you have to do is pick a side. If you like miniskirts, the beach and ski resorts (with no more than forty-five minutes in between) you can join a group of Lebanese and help them in their sacred quest of 'enjoying and celebrating the love of life'. Beirut, however, is no Western city so if you are chasing the discreet yet violent and evasive charm of the East, or fighting the big evil imperialism (intellectually or violently), you will find a lot of stories and tales to indulge your ears in this newly self-proclaimed victorious city that is neither completely Eastern or Western.

History has stopped repeating in Beirut, it has become ridiculous and vulgar for even the names are the same in this urbanity where wars, conflicts and spectacular assassinations are just a part of the loop. How do you cope with that? How can you still party and live? What is the secret? How can you make all this coherent? One word: Denial.

Beirut has always been an obvious surprise, a place that feels too weird to mature, and too rare to disappear, bearing its open scars while being occupied by by legions of Peter Pans.

This reduces our guide to something closer to a tipster. The only sure way to get to know Beirut is to come here and compile your own views.

So if you do that one day, please do enjoy my city; and try not to smoke.

MOMENTUM

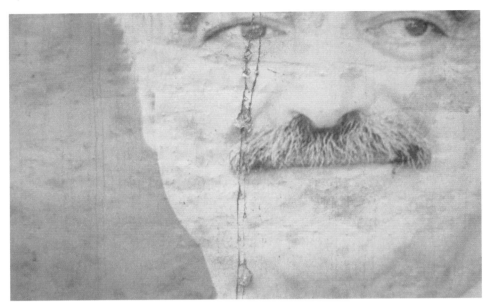

Photos by Jan Rothuizen

The assassination of former Prime Minister Rafik Hariri, in 2005, may look like the pinnacle event of contemporary Lebanon due to the changes and divide it brought about in the country. Yet many Beirutis would ask, 'What about the events of 1975, 1982, 1989, 1990, 1993, 1996, 2000, 2006, 2008...?' These are all historical moments, which are loaded with political meaning. Typically in Beirut, these events are propagated by political and religious posters and used extensively as ideological territory markers throughout the city.

After Hariri's assassination on Valentine's Day 2005, and again after Hezbollah overtook the capital's streets in May 2008, a war of posters broke out in the streets of Beirut. These posters can be understood as the city's most visual barometer of the political situation at large.

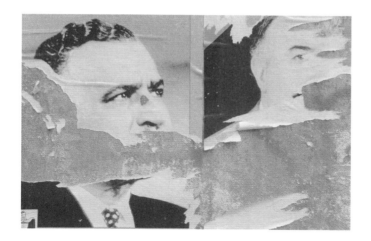

OVER A CUP OF COFFEE

Does touring Beirut's monuments of assassinations become palatable while sipping coffee? We are about to find out.

AN ASSASSINATION TOUR IN BEIRUT

Beirut has a dark side that is still moved by violent currents flowing beneath the surface of the city. The Civil War officially ended in the early 1990s, but the powers that animated it are still roaming, holding between them thin lines that uphold a delicate stability. This equilibrium, if disturbed, will often realign itself with a 'short' spurt of violence, taking the form of assassinations of political figures, small clashes or even mini civil wars. Awareness regarding these facts is necessary and has become part of the local mindset. The assassination tour takes on mainly tragic events that physically affected the city and the urban surroundings. In the places you will be led to, the aftermath of these attempts contributed to the proliferation of public spaces and gardens. Unfortunately, and strangely enough, assassinations have

become an elementary force in the contemporary spatial and urban development of Beirut. As such, in a city torn apart in war and peace for the last three decades, death is a common ground capable of preserving the public space, and plays a major role in 'planning' the future of the city. This tour will point these places out to you so you can experience the spaces, and will tell you about other martyr-related buildings along the way.

MARTYRS' SQUARE

is in the oldest part of Beirut. This square is a commemoration of the martyrs of 1916. In those days, the different communities in the territory that is now Lebanon had a common enemy, the Ottomans. Fighting occupation and starvation, the peoples of this land had every reason to show solidarity, and even started to act as one

It is one of the few places in Lebanon that escaped religious or community connotations. It was a no-man's-land during the Civil War.

society. Although the martyrs were both Muslim and Christian, they all died for a dream called Lebanon, but their vision had very different interpretations to each community. This difference in points of view included the official burial of the Martyrs of 1916 which had a controversial story. The Ottomans threw the Martyrs in a mass grave. On their defeat and the invasion by the French, the leaders wanted to honor these Martyrs with a proper burial as a way of showing their good intentions towards the locals. Their plans were to establish a common resting place. No religious group, except the Druze, agreed to donate land in Beirut for that purpose. It is interesting to note that the martyrs were Christians and Muslims. None were Druze. Martyrs' Square is one of the few places in Lebanon that escaped religious or community connotations. It was a no-man's-land during the Civil War. A state square and proper public space, so to speak. As of late, the ownership by a private real estate company, a huge mosque, and the final resting place of late Prime Minister Hariri, contest this fact.

AL KAMAL BUILDING,

on Monot Street, is also a hidden war relic, standing between several restored high-rise buildings. Destroyed inside and out, full of bullet holes from light-weight

weapons, it is said that gun fights used to take place inside of the building, from floor to floor, and from one room to another.

BASHIR EL GEMAYEL

born in 1947, was assassinated in 1982 by a massive explosion. He had just been elected President. Coming from a political family, he was head of the Christian militia that controlled East Beirut. Hero and upholder of the Christian dream to some, thug and criminal to other communities in Lebanon, this perception made him no different from any other political and military personalities in Lebanon.

SASSINE SQUARE

is located in the heart of Ashrafieh, with a monument erected in the memory of Bashir El Gemayel, not far from the spot on which he was assassinated. It does not look

like a square, but it is as busy as any square, with cafés and restaurants all around it. The environment and people of the area protect the monument, for the death of Gemayel is still very much alive. Just ask.

BARAKAT BUILDING

was designed by Youssef Aftimus in 1920. It was not its shape that was to contribute to its fame, but its location on a strategic point on the Green Line. One of the last relics on these demarcation lines of the Lebanese Civil War, the scars of this building were saved by a stubborn hairdresser, only to become a war museum.

SAMIR KASSIR (1960-2005) & GEBRAN TUENI (1957-2006)

were a journalist (scholar and historian) and a chief editor, respectively, of Annahar newspaper (established 1933). They worked together in Annahar building in downtown Beirut, and now their memorials, in a quiet square with two fig trees and a commemorative monument, also face each other beside that same building. So what is mightier, the pen or the sword?

HOLIDAY INN & MURR TOWER

It was said that in order to win the war of Beirut, you have to take two buildings, the Holiday Inn and the Murr Tower. These landmarks are still war relics, but the Holiday Inn has an extra something, it was considered the symbol of Western imperialism.

GENERAL FRANCOIS HAJJ (1953-2007)

became famous after leading the fight between the Lebanese Army against the Fateh Al Islam armed group in the north of Lebanon. A bomb took his life and a street in Beirut was named after him.

BASSEL FLEIHAN (1963-2005)

a Member of Parliament, was assassinated alongside Rafik Hariri in a massive explosion. A modest memorial was installed at the top of the St. Georges road leading to the spot where he was assassinated.

RAFIK HARIRI (1944-2005)

was a Member of Parliament at the time of his assassination, but he had also been Prime Minister, and was 'Mr. Lebanon' to his partisans. A series of events took place after his demise, including the withdrawal of Syrian troops from Lebanon. Many monuments were erected to commemorate Rafik Hariri. Apart from his final resting place at Martyrs' Square, there is a monument dedicated to him in the Serail (government palace) but the most famous is located at the spot of the assassination, in front of the St. Georges Hotel, a piece

of real estate in Beirut that he tried to acquire but could not. A garden commemorating all his accomplishments, and singing flags remind us of the 1,000 kilos of TNT used to assassinate Rafik Hariri. It was the 14 February, Valentine's Day.

A few meters and you will have the sea, it is Manara. Enjoy.

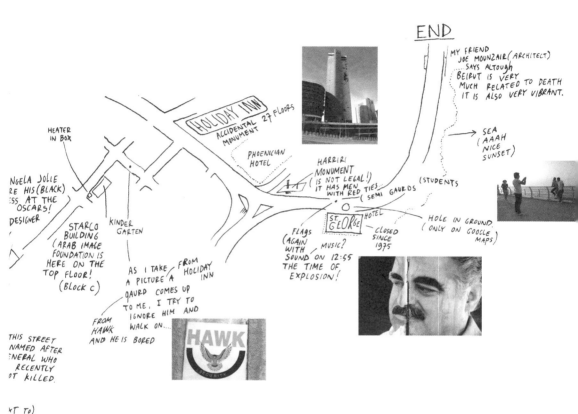

END

MY FRIEND
JOE MOUNZAIR (ARCHITECT)
SAYS ALTOUGH
BEIRUT IS VERY
MUCH RELATED TO DEATH
IT IS ALSO VERY VIBRANT.

HOLIDAY INN
ACCIDENTAL MONUMENT 27 FLOORS

HEATER
IN BOX

SEA
(AAAH
NICE
SUNSET)

PHOENICIAN
HOTEL

HARRIRI
MONUMENT
(IS NOT LEGAL!)
IT HAS MEN
WITH RED TIES (SEMI GAURDS

(STUDENTS

NGELA JOLIE
2E HIS (BLACK)
SS AT THE
OSCARS!
DESIGNER

STARCO
BUILDING
(ARAB IMAGE
FOUNDATION IS
HERE ON THE
TOP FLOOR!
(BLOCK C)

KINDER
GARTEN

ST.
GEORGE HOTEL

- CLOSED
SINCE
1975

HOLE IN GROUND.
(ONLY ON GOOGLE
MAPS)

FLAGS
(AGAIN
WITH
SOUND ON 12:55
THE TIME OF
EXPLOSION!

MUSIC?

AS I TAKE
A PICTURE A
GAURD COMES UP
TO ME, I TRY TO
IGNORE HIM AND
WALK ON....

FROM
HOLIDAY
INN

FROM
HAWK
AND HE IS BORED

HAWK
SECURITY

THIS STREET
NAMED AFTER
:NERAL WHO
RECENTLY
OT KILLED.

×T TO)
OF
EE

Map by Jan Rothuizen

A-B-C
The science of
everyday life in Beirut

A city-law in Beirut, be it for traffic, zoning or building typology, has the status not of a legal object but of a secular text: it is subject to interpretation, to the extent to which we can say that individuals use the laws as a domain of self-expression. Discover the rules of navigation and then observe behavior.

If we take a cross-section of any area of the city and observe it for some hours, we are very likely to find a variety of occurrences which can be considered as standard patterns repeated in the city:

A. A hole somewhere in the surface of the asphalted street • **B.** A programmed power cut • **C.** A variety of people in many households watching the Turkish television series Nour • **D.** A recently renovated sidewalk that is at such a high level that it even requires considerable effort from cats to jump up from street level • **E.** A building under construction, promising on its billboard a classy finish: extra marble for a glossy effect • **F.** If we make sure that our section is deep enough to cut into the subsoil we might also find some pieces or remains of other, often Roman, cities • **G.** A sudden interruption or significant narrowing of the sidewalk because a building takes up too much space in the street • **H.** A shop selling vegetables • **I.** Music from the local pop radio station • **J.** The smell of good home cooking • **K.** Some loud television news that points out that you are either with... or with... • **L.** One bottle-blonde • **M.** One 'siliconed' woman • **N.** A guy looking at some parts of the blonde or of the siliconed woman (he also looks at brunettes, nobody should worry) • **O.** A gas station and a shop selling cars, car parts or for car repairs • **P.** People saying hello from car to car, from sidewalk to sidewalk, from square to square • **Q.** Bip bip bip bip (someone driving an official car and the non-stop noise in everyday life) • **R.** Sandwich shop with a smell of something frying (perhaps not downtown) • **S.** An intersection where people are not yet sure if they should follow the policeman or the traffic signs for guidance • **T.** Somebody driving convinced that his/her phone conversation is very important, more important than the pedestrian crossing the street at a random spot • **U.** A valet parking 'official', the king of the street, the person who at the same time is generating traffic jams and organizing private traffic to private places • **V.** A motorcycle always in a hurry and using the 'Chinese path' (never straight) to drive between cars • **W.** An old BMW (1980s?) whose driver seems intent on killing somebody without having to answer for it • **X.** Some cockroaches passing by • **Y.** Some concierges cleaning the entrances of buildings • **Z.** Sun •

WHAT NOT TO DO IF YOU HEAR AN EXPLOSION:

Car bombs, explosions, skirmishes and small clashes have been frequent in Beirut for more than three decades now. After thirty years of this 'routine' people have developed a series of precautions that sometimes have the opposite effect.

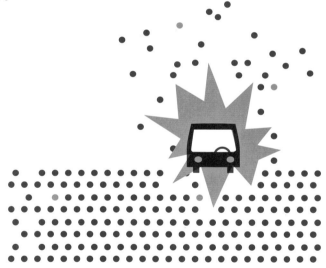

Illustration by Pascale Harès

- Don't panic
- Don't call anyone
- Don't turn on the TV or the radio
- If you turn on the TV, don't read the news bar – it will suck in your brain
- Don't try to understand what or why this has happened
- Don't worry
- Don't be happy

20

FAST PERSPECTIVES ON BEIRUT

A rapid-fire questionnaire is often the most telling way to fight the clichés and collage a true first impression.

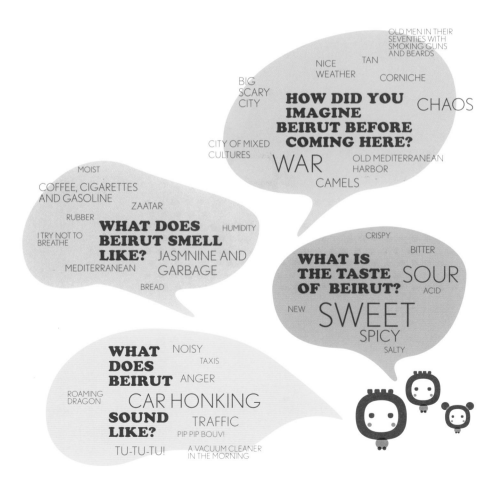

HOW DID YOU IMAGINE BEIRUT BEFORE COMING HERE?
OLD MEN IN THEIR SEVENTIES WITH SMOKING GUNS AND BEARDS
NICE WEATHER
TAN
CORNICHE
BIG SCARY CITY
CHAOS
CITY OF MIXED CULTURES
WAR
OLD MEDITERRANEAN HARBOR
CAMELS

WHAT DOES BEIRUT SMELL LIKE?
MOIST
COFFEE, CIGARETTES AND GASOLINE
ZAATAR
RUBBER
HUMIDITY
I TRY NOT TO BREATHE
JASMNINE AND GARBAGE
MEDITERRANEAN
BREAD

WHAT IS THE TASTE OF BEIRUT?
CRISPY
BITTER
SOUR
ACID
NEW
SWEET
SPICY
SALTY

WHAT DOES BEIRUT SOUND LIKE?
NOISY
TAXIS
ANGER
ROAMING DRAGON
CAR HONKING
TRAFFIC
PIP PIP BOUV!
TU-TU-TU!
A VACUUM CLEANER IN THE MORNING

Illustration by Pascale Harès

TAKE TAXIS

BE CHAOTIC

EAT ANYTIME

WHAT IS THE THING YOU WOULD NOT DO IN YOUR COUNTRY BUT YOU DO IT IN BEIRUT?

LISTEN TO LEBANESE MUSIC

SMOKE DURING DINNER

NOT FOLLOW MAPS

BE A REBEL

DRIVE ON THE WRONG SIDE OF THE STREET

MULTILINGUAL

SHOPS

ALCOHOLISM

COOL PEOPLE

WHAT DOES BEIRUT HAVE IN COMMON WITH YOUR CITY?

RAIN

BUMS

IT'S A CITY

PARTY PEOPLE

NIGHTILFE

UNPREDICTABLE

IF BEIRUT WERE A VIDEOGAME, WHAT WOULD YOU CONSIDER IT TO BE?

VERY HARD

TRICKY

DANGEROUSLY ADDICTIVE

SEA

WORK

CURIOSITY

FRIENDS

WHY DID YOU VISIT BEIRUT THE FIRST TIME?

FUN

FAMILY

INTERESTING

VACATION

DANGER

ADDICTION

I NEVER LEFT

JOB

WHY WOULD YOU COME BACK?

PEOPLE

INSPIRATION

TO LIVE

FRIENDS

DIVERSITY

ACTION

PURPLE

RED

GREY

BLACK BECAUSE IT HAS A MIX OF ALL COLORS

IF BEIRUT WERE A COLOR WHAT WOULD IT BE?

YELLOW

BEIGE

WHITE

BROWN COFFEE

BLUE

NOTHING

I CAN'T LIVE IN 2 PLACES AT THE SAME TIME

IT'S JUST GREAT

NO BUTS

BEIRUT IS A GREAT CITY BUT...

SOME STUPID FUCKERS SHOT AT IT

TOO MANY HIGH BUILDINGS, TOO LITTLE GREEN SPOTS

WALLAW

HOMMOS

AHLAN

KHALLAS

WHAT ARE THE LEBANESE WORDS YOU KNOW?

SHARMOOTA

HABIBI

SHUKRAN

YALLA

EVERYBODY

GOD

IF BEIRUT WERE A MASTERPIECE, WHO WOULD BE THE ARTIST?

TIME

HISTORY

FEYROUZ

THE TURKS, THE FRENCH, THE PERSIANS

THE PEOPLE

A first impression of a city like Beirut might be chaotic and overwhelming. Is this place like the images we saw elsewhere? Are the people as we expected? The first Lebanese things we see, smell and hear interact with our knowledge of the place but also our expectations and pre-conceptions. Your senses are challenged to bring order to all these impressions. Then you need to navigate through unknown Beirut with all its differences and sometimes similarities to your home. You search for landmarks, entry points, public transport destinations; you try to recognize main streets, building façades and storefronts. You feel the odd one out, the tourist with the camera, and you try to familiarize yourself with basic local habits of walking, greeting and driving.

BUILDINGS   Place de L'Etoile   MONUMENTS   The Murr Tower   PLANNING   The Absence of It

INFRASTRUCTURE   The Corniche   TRADE + SERVICES   No Backpackers Hostel in Town!

Photo by Jeannette Gaussi

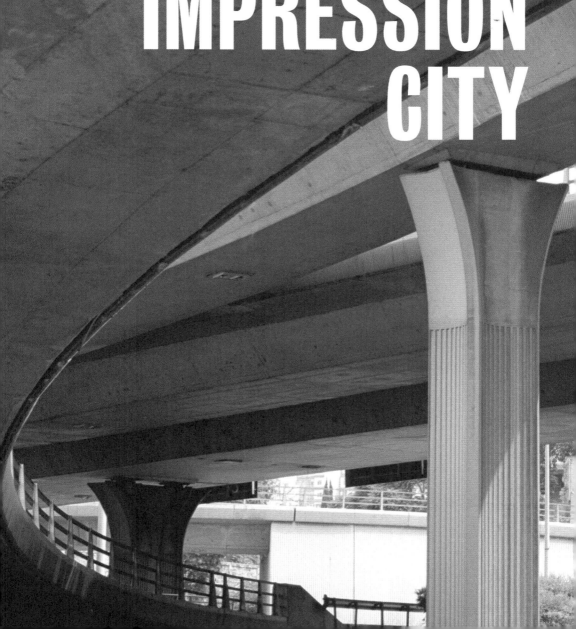

FIRST
IMPRESSION
CITY

Michael Stanton

TERRAIN VAGUE

An attempt to piece together the anomaly of Solidere and the cyclical reinvention of downtown Beirut.

The lack of value evident in most new building in metropolitan Beirut and in other cities in Lebanon has promoted interest in that which is not yet built, in the *terrain vague* at the center of the capital. The void produced is indeed radical and does present both extreme provocation and great possibility. At the end of the Civil War, the government facilitated Rafik Hariri's vision for rebuilding the downtown by consolidating all properties in the center except those with religious immunity and by then offering shares[1] in the corporation for its development. A law passed in December 1991 gave the munici-

1   Shares were first offered to owners of property in the affected area, then to the government, then to the public and finally to interested Arab neighbors. $650 Million was thus amassed.

pal administration the authority to create real estate companies in war-damaged areas, and to entrust them with the implementation of the urban plan and the promotion, marketing, and sale of properties to individual or corporate developers... Thus shares will, in effect, replace title deeds of ownership.'[2] Multiple ownership was replaced with a single entity but a publicly-owned one, in the sense that it sold stock. This peculiar transference, from private property to public, but within a cor-

2   Assam Salem, 'The Role of Government in Shaping the Built Environment,' In: Peter G. Rowe and Hashim Sarkis (ed.), *Projecting Beirut; Episodes in the Construction and Reconstruction of a Modern City* (Prestel 1998), pp. 131.

porate frame, is one of the general paradoxes of capitalism, but in Beirut it took on a more emphatic and asset-based character

than in other circumstances, for it pertained to control of the center of a capital city. Solidere was thus appointed, but was so integral in the mechanisms ordaining its appointment that any a priori objective, governmental role is ambiguous. When Hariri, the corporation's leader, attained the nation's most powerful political position, that of Prime Minister, this process was augmented and coincided with the demolition of most of the downtown.

As many as two thousand buildings disappeared. Some were undamaged and are still inhabited. Many were recoverable. Others were truly beyond restoration, especially along the Green Line, the no-man's-land that had divided the city during fifteen years of fighting. The extreme actions that had typified the war thus continued in the development process, both in the destruction and in the amalgam of commerce and administration that oversaw its rebuilding. Extreme land values crossed with changes in commercial demographics: a formula that produces the empty downtowns in the U.S., where surface parking stretches between the towers, has shaped a similar fabric in Beirut. Nowadays it has the aspect of Houston's empty core, an expectant void. Likewise the other 'downtowns' that cluster at the crossing points of vehicular traffic around Houston are similar to new satellite cores like Kaslik, which formed in the Christian enclave during the Civil War, and others that stretch along the fifty kilometers of coast that the metropolis now amalgamates.

With the excuse of speed or the incompetence of the collective, the downtown was consolidated and homogenized. 250,000 owners were made stockholders in the single entity that replaced them. The cult of efficiency, a familiar pretext for the centralizing forces of capitalism (which must systematically increase revenues each year) met the spatial totalitarianism to which the market aspires: monopoly and state incorporated. Beirut's problems may stem from the simple fact that almost the whole downtown now has one owner. This may be unique in the capitalist world. While large parts of East Berlin, Warsaw, Stalingrad or Beijing were radically eviscerated and reconstructed as state showplaces, this sort of total urbanism usually remains impossible, even in the most extreme cases of market capitalism. In Beirut, the formula of State-Socialist hyper-tableaux was implemented for antithetical economic reasons to those that made the Stalinist total theater of the Lenin Allees.

Yet chaos, as embodied in multiple ownership, is what cities are. The struggle of desire and fact makes a metropolitan pressure and formal mix. The sterility of downtown Beirut stems directly from its ownership practices and the codes established for its reconstruction. It now manifests a bourgeois notion of urban quality, uniformly dainty and over-restored – 'like a rhinestone-encrusted beige poodle clipped too perfectly.'[3] No vulgar signage, no mobile vendors as were characteristic of this central quarter before the war and as are typical in other nearby Arab cities like Damascus or Tripoli. Any reference to the 5,000-year history of the city is reduced to archaeology from Phoenician and Roman times, or must rest in the religious buildings of all ages that were protected by waqf restrictions providing automatic exemption for all

3   Michael Stanton, 'The Good, the Bad and the Ugly: Urbanism and Intention', *Volume* no. 11 (2007), p. 97.

ecclesiastical structures, for worship or otherwise, from state action. Large areas of prime urban land

---

...downtown Beirut, now manifests a bourgeois notion of urban quality, uniformly dainty and over-restored - 'like a rhinestone-encrusted beige poodle clipped too perfectly'.

---

throughout the city and nation are thus 'protected'. The concept behind waqf is that of universality, that all religious structures are owned by the sum of adherents to the faith they represent.

Thus a mosque, cathedral or even a school is the property of millions. This has more than a passing similarity to the ambiguous attitude to property displayed by Solidere as a publicly-owned entity, or in fact in all corporations that offer stock. This particular form of property immunity is one of the few examples of the separation of religion and state. Mosques, churches, Druze houses and a synagogue now sit isolated in the enormous vacant lot that is most of the downtown. This municipal installation-piece emphasizes the hierarchies that determine Lebanese life, both the dominance of religion as a cultural determinant and the hetero-sectarianism that is the nation's gift. This gift constitutes automatic multi-cultural possibilities, and the nation's curse, in the way that sectarianism has been used to separate and discriminate culminating in the perpetual violence of which the Civil War appeared to be the last horrendous episode. Though it was superseded by the war between Hezbollah and Israel and then the ensuing political show-down again revived active confessional hostilities. Religion continues its primacy as a determining force in Lebanese culture in the physical zoning of its cities.

Among projects in the area, the construction of an enormous new mosque on Martyrs' Square has been the most extravagant gesture so far. The mosque's construction was taken over directly by Hariri. With an imposing dome and four minarets, it defies the modest typologies of historic Lebanese religious structures and, along with another huge mosque in Hariri's home town of Saida, introduces an imperial scale to this sort of architecture, conflating religion and regime. The Beirut building recalls Sinan and the great mosques of Istanbul, and in Saida the Mamluk heritage of Cairo serves as the reference. The Beirut mosque also sits next to, and overshadows, the Maronite Catholic cathedral. Since Hariri's death and unusual entombment along with his bodyguards [4] in the plaza next to the building and adjacent to Martyrs' Square, this has become the site of the continuing protests and mourning that have altered the Lebanese political fabric. Vast crowds now fill the voids that were created with the evisceration of the downtown after the Civil War. Martyrs' Square, a long rectangular plaza reminiscent of Rome's Piazza Navona in proportion and significance, and one of the most important civic spaces and circulation nodes in pre-war Beirut, lost its defining edge of buildings and is part of this huge empty zone of epic proportions in which one million citizens were able to gather in a decisive independence rally in March 2005. It appears that 25% of the entire population of the nation descended on this site.

This process of the replacement of expensive but vacant real estate with throngs had already begun at the beginning of this millennium when Solidere, realizing that the vision of an exclusive up-scale shopping and social quarter was not taking off, encouraged more popular businesses to temporarily occupy unrented stores. A heterogeneous crowd was invited into a downtown transformed into a vibrant souk. 'Festival' replaced more conventional notions of commerce and has continued in both pro-Western and pro-Iranian/Syrian events. Most office space remains empty but shops and restaurants, often of the up-scale sort originally envisioned for the area, have subsequently moved in and at least the ground floors of buildings are active. A cross-section of Beiruti society, some merely spectators prohibited by economic difference from actually participating in retail activity, some the imagined haute-bourgeoisie that the area was originally intended to host, is augmented by a blend of visitors and tourists, mostly from the Arab countries, who were flooding Lebanon physically and revitalizing it economically before the recent war and subsequent conflicts intimidated many of them.

'Event' has replaced conventional urban ensemble in the city center. Now energy is multiplied exponentially by the demonstrations and apparatus that accompany the political crises still swirling since the murder of Solidere's founder. The fact that the current revolutionary political events were triggered by the death of the region's greatest real estate tycoon is not merely a coincidence. The melding of property development with the most intrinsic civic structures is a component of all late-capitalist space, but in Lebanon it becomes an overriding issue. Hariri's loss is then a civic sacrifice whose legacy has both reified and transcended the fascinating folly that is the empty heart of Beirut.

4   Usually, Muslim burial is prescribed for very specific sites and this spot, opposite the door of the mosque outside in public space, is not one of those spots. Unlike the Christian habit of erecting tombs and monuments, Islam, with its reluctance toward the cult of immortal personality and physical representation is more loath to commemorate in such an explicit manner. Exceptions are made for especially heroic or holy figures such as the tomb of Salah'din at the entrance of the Umayyad mosque in Damascus. Hariri's grave appears to be one of the first of such exceptions made in Lebanon and it places him within a very exalted pantheon. Given that he is interred and in Martyr's Square in front of the mosque that was to form his religious center-piece for Beirut and that he has posthumously become such a talisman for change, this very quick decision does hold with greater deliberation. One million seems a safe estimate for the attendance at this definitive opposition gathering. Given that at least 90% of those attending were Lebanese, even more if long-time Palestinian residents of Lebanon are not included, this may have been as much as a quarter of the entire population of the nation!

A CHEAP DAY TOUR IN BEIRUT

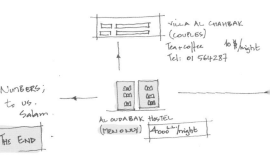

VILLA AL CHAHBAK
(COUPLES)
Tea + coffee   10 $/night
Tel: 01 564287

Got BETTER NUMBERS;
Send them to us.
              Salam.

AL OUDABAK HOSTEL
(MEN ONLY)   1000 L.L./night

THE END

A full but CHEAP DAY IN BEIRUT

$1 € = 2000$ L.L.

$1 \$ = 1500$ L.L.

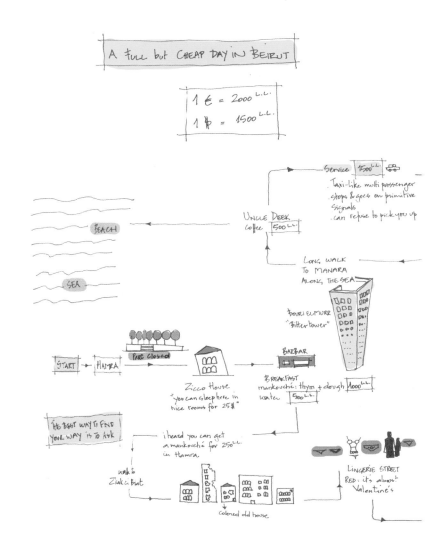

Service   1500 L.L.
. Taxi-like multi passenger
 stops & goes on primitive
 signals
. can refuse to pick you up

UNCLE DEEK
coffee   500 L.L.

BEACH

SEA

LONG WALK
TO MANARA
ALONG THE SEA

BOURS ELMURR
"Bitter tower"

BARBAR
BREAKFAST
mankouchè: thym + dough 1000 L.L.
water   500 L.L.

START → HAMRA

PARC Closed

Zicco House
"you can sleep here in
nice rooms for 25$"

THE BEST WAY TO FIND
YOUR WAY IS TO ASK

i heard you can get
a mankouchè for 250 L.L.
in Hamra.

walk to
Zkak el Blat

colored old house

LINGERIE STREET
RED: it's almost
Valentine's

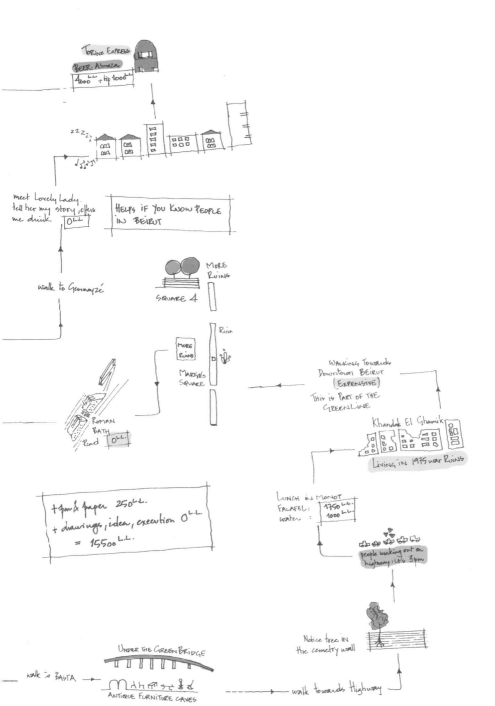

Torino Express

BEER: Almaza

4000 + tip 1000

zzzz

meet lovely lady.
tell her my story, offers
me drink   0 L.L.

HELPS IF YOU KNOW PEOPLE
IN BEIRUT

walk to Gemmayzé

MORE
RUINS

SQUARE 4

Ruin

MORE
RUINS

MARTYR'S
SQUARE

ROMAN
BATH
Road   0 L.L.

WALKING TOWARDS
DOWNTOWN BEIRUT
(EXPENSIVE)
THIS IS PART OF THE
GREENLINE

Khandak El Ghamik

LIVING IN 1975 war Ruins

+ pen & paper 250 L.L.
+ drawings, idea, execution 0 L.L.
= 15500 L.L.

LUNCH IN MONOT
FALAFEL: 1750 L.L.
WATER :   1000 L.L.

people making out on
highway : it's 3 pm

Notice tree IN
the cemetery wall

UNDER THE GREEN BRIDGE

walk to BASTA

ANTIQUE FURNITURE CAVES

walk towards Highway

URBAN MYTHS

In a city where nothing is certain and rumors and hearsay are all you have to go by, myths become sacred wisdom.

Illustration by Pascale Harès

In the 1970s a group of brilliant Lebanese scientists gathered in Bourj Hammoud, the Armenian neighborhood in East Beirut, to build a rocket that could fly to the moon. They chose Bourj Hammoud because it was an industrial area. They could use the skills of all the electricians, metalworkers and other handymen who worked in the area. After its launch the rocket, named ARZ 1 (Cedar 1), flew briefly before plummeting into the Mediterranean. Sabotage by the CIA or MOSSAD was suspected.

Bashir El Gemayel, the assassinated president of Lebanon, is claimed to be alive. Shortly after the explosion on Sassine Square, a helicopter was seen leaving the site for an unknown destination. The helicopter was said to be carrying Bashir Gemayel. It is widely believed that he now lives in a safe haven near Buenos Aires, Argentina, where he spends his days playing golf with Elvis and Dr. Mengele.

Shortly after the Israeli War in 2006 they stumbled upon a totally carbonized tree that still grew new leaves and new flowers. It was believed to be a holy tree. Now people can visit the holy tree in Beit Jbeil or some other southern village.

A rich guy in Rabieh, an eastern suburb of Beirut, had a 'thing' for reptiles. After he imported a Komodo dragon, the beast went AWOL on a dark and gloomy night. It is said that the reptile still wanders the hills surrounding Rabieh and feeds on stray cats, little children and small rodents.

The Abu Armstrong family emigrated from Basta, a neighborhood south of the Old City, to Boston USA, somewhere in the early nineteen-hundreds. One of the great grandchildren, a bloke called Neil Armstrong, went to the moon and planted the Lebanese flag a short distance away from the US flag. The television footage was clearly tampered with. After returning to Earth he moved back to his ancestral house in Basta and became a Sunni Muslim.

In 2003 Lebanese scientists found the third biggest oilfield just off the coast of Byblos. The secret faction in the Lebanese government concealed the discovery in order to save the global environment. (The same happened to the discovery of gold in the Bekaa – so the price of gold would not take a nosedive – and the discovery of uranium in the south, which was kept secret to not upset the Iranians).

CORNICHE WALKING MAP

Losing your way in the streets of Hamra ...

Map by Jan Rothuizen

RAOUCHE

Most Beirut guidebooks will feature Pigeon Rocks. Do you want to know the real stories of this iconic place?

In every guide book of Beirut you will find the so called Pigeon Rocks. They are located along the shore of a part of Beirut called Raouche. The rocks are actually two islands, one with a more feminine shape, including a hole through which you can sail, through swim under and jump off. The other is more like a phallus standing in the water. Looking at this phallus from a boat, some buildings of the high-rise waterfront of this part of Beirut make this Pigeon Rock appear even longer! Together the feminine rock and the phallus rock look like a couple standing in the water, maybe holding hands under the surface of the Mediterranean. Perhaps this is the reason the place is called Pigeon Rocks, calling to mind the Dutch word 'tortelduifjes', which means lovebirds.

Along the same shore, next to those two small islands, there is a peninsula, which is also part of Raouche. Together with a large beach called Ramlet al Bayda (a bit more to the south), these two beautiful parts along Beirut's boulevard (the Corniche) are the only 'natural' spots left of the city's central coastline. Natural in the sense that there are no, or very few, concrete structures. Also natural in the sense that, on the peninsula, sheep are grazing, grass is growing and just a few cars are driving around. People live in wooden sheds and little stone houses. While on the other side of the Corniche development is taking place, and more and more huge flats are shooting up. This contrast, together with its beautiful environment, makes the peninsula of Raouche a great place to be, and live.

SOME HISTORY OF RAOUCHE

Today some 200 people live on this piece of land; they walk around in much the same way as people walked through Beirut a long time ago. This is one of Beirut's romantic hideouts and had in fact already been 'discovered' a century ago, by nobody less than Thomas Edward Lawrence, alias Lawrence of Arabia. Oral history, as recounted by some of the Sunni population of the peninsula, contains well known romantic stories about Lawrence and his friend Selim Ahmed spending time on the peninsula, watching the Raouche rocks and holding hands. Apparently, a famous photograph which Lawrence took of Selim Ahmed, was taken at Raouche. Besides being a romantic place, Raouche is famous for its natural harbors. Especially on the south side of the peninsula there are harbors not only used by fisherman, couples or sunbathers, but for more serious, illegal, purposes. At the archaeological museum of the American University

Photos by Cleo Campert

of Beirut an old inhabitant of Beirut was very clear about the covert function of the small natural harbor on the south side. Until about fifty years ago, the place was used by smugglers. Since this was a very remote area of Beirut during that period, the place was perfect to bring in all kinds of merchandise. According to the fisherman now living here, the smuggling stopped a long time ago... Alhamdulillah.

On the north side of this peninsula, with its fifty, mostly wooden houses, there is also a harbor, but this one is at the bottom of a five meter high cliff. The inhabitants have built small 'cranes' by filling empty oil tanks with concrete. With these crane-constructions they can lower their boats into the water to empty their nets. The youngest of the family living in this part of Raouche sails tourists or 'lovebirds' past the Pigeon Rocks, so don't forget to bring your bathing suit.

As fishermen, these people can be categorized as hunters and gatherers. Besides that, they are specialized in fixing polyester boats.

THE HERO OF RAOUCHE

The real treasure of Raouche is the Batal el Raouche, or the 'Hero of Raouche'. This hero is a huge guy with a big beard. Inside his wooden house (which

blew away during a recent autumn storm and was re-built thanks to a donation by the Hariri family) he lies on a mattress and tells beautiful stories, in Arabic. He is called the Hero of Raouche because he has jumped off the Rouche cliffs some forty or fifty times to save the lives of some of the people who try to jump to their deaths each year.

From an anthropological point of view this man is the shaman of the tribe. In keeping with oral tradition, he can tell you the local history and anecdotes. Stories about the period when there was more agriculture, details about his tribe being robbed by Palestinians, fishing stories, about cliff jumping (of course) and about the grass growing on the peninsula, about the other families, the boats, the couples and his wife and children.

If you decide to visit this (small) part of Beirut, go and find this man. Take him a piece of Dutch cheese (which he likes a lot) and bring someone who speaks Arabic, sit down and listen...

If there was a treasure map of Raouche than this man is the box of gold.

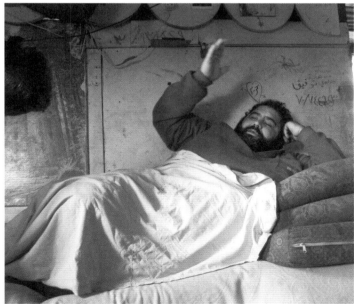

38 MAYFLOWER HOTEL

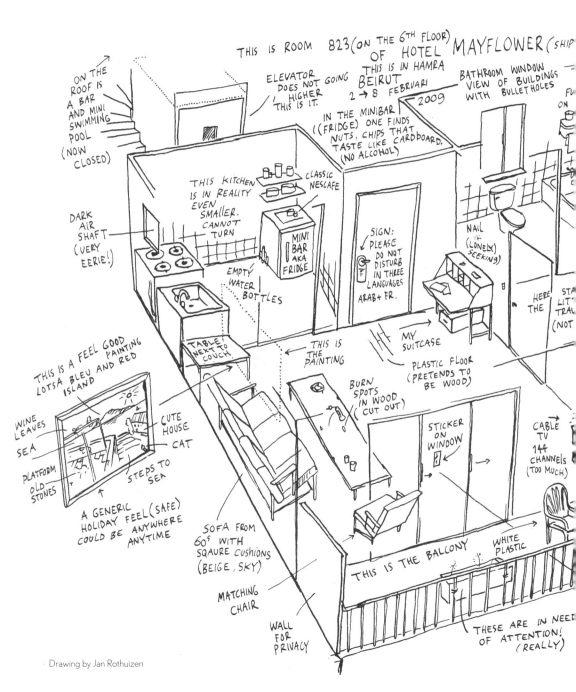

THIS IS ROOM 823 (ON THE 6TH FLOOR) OF HOTEL MAYFLOWER (SHIP

THIS IS IN HAMRA BEIRUT

ELEVATOR DOES NOT GOING HIGHER THIS IS IT.

2 → 8 FEBRUARI 2009

BATHROOM WINDOW VIEW OF BUILDINGS WITH BULLETHOLES

ON THE ROOF IS A BAR AND MINI SWIMMING POOL (NOW CLOSED)

IN THE MINIBAR ((FRIDGE) ONE FINDS NUTS, CHIPS THAT TASTE LIKE CARDBOARD. (NO ALCOHOL)

THIS KITCHEN IS IN REALITY EVEN SMALLER. CANNOT TURN

CLASSIC NESCAFE

DARK AIR SHAFT (VERY EERIE!)

MINI BAR AKA FRIDGE

NAIL (LONELY SEEKING)

SIGN: PLEASE DO NOT DISTURB IN THREE LANGUAGES ARAB + FR.

EMPTY WATER BOTTLES

HERE THE

STA LIT TRA (NOT

THIS IS A FEEL GOOD PAINTING LOTSA BLEU AND RED ISLAND

TABLE NEXT TO COUCH

THIS IS THE PAINTING

MY SUITCASE

PLASTIC FLOOR (PRETENDS TO BE WOOD)

WINE LEAVES

SEA

CUTE HOUSE

CAT

BURN SPOTS IN WOOD (CUT OUT)

STICKER ON WINDOW

CABLE TV 144 CHANNELS (TOO MUCH)

PLATFORM OLD STONES

STEPS TO SEA

A GENERIC HOLIDAY FEEL (SAFE) COULD BE ANYWHERE ANYTIME

SOFA FROM 60s WITH SQAURE CUSHIONS (BEIGE, SKY)

THIS IS THE BALCONY

WHITE PLASTIC

MATCHING CHAIR

WALL FOR PRIVACY

THESE ARE IN NEED OF ATTENTION! (REALLY)

Drawing by Jan Rothuizen

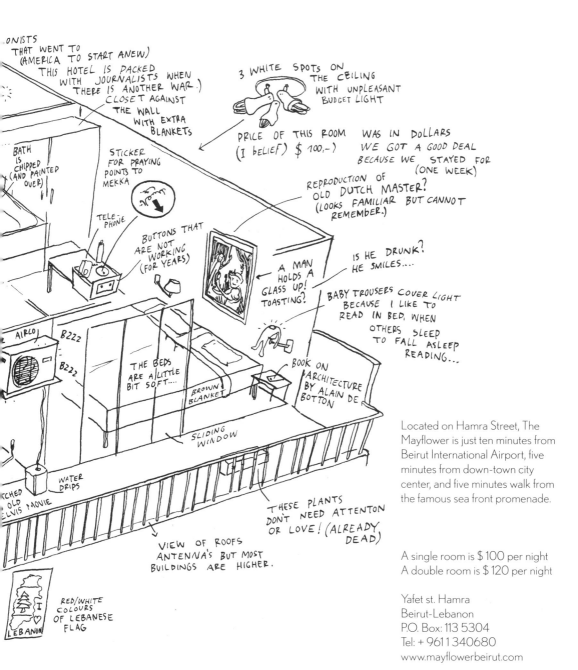

Located on Hamra Street, The Mayflower is just ten minutes from Beirut International Airport, five minutes from down-town city center, and five minutes walk from the famous sea front promenade.

A single room is $ 100 per night
A double room is $ 120 per night

Yafet st. Hamra
Beirut-Lebanon
P.O. Box: 113 5304
Tel: + 961 1 340680
www.mayflowerbeirut.com

TO DAHIYA

An inside look at the cheapest way to enter Dahiya. Bus no. 4
is an easy and accessible means of public transportation.

Photos by Elias Moubarak

HEZBOLLAH'S WHITE ROOM

Joost Janmaat

About 3.5 by 4 meters, low ceiling at about 2.10 meters. Walls whitewashed with acrylic paint (washable?), sockets for **ELECTRICITY** and internet in all walls, cheap dark-blue **SYNTHETIC CARPET**. Two windows set with frosted, **WIRE-ENFORCED GLASS** and thick bars. Four non-matching chairs against the far wall, a small square table between chairs two and three, ashtray on top. In the middle of the room a firm plywood desk, with a half-open box on top allowing the interrogator to write things down unseen. The only decorative element in the room is the little brass oval around the door lock.

Photos by Elias Moubarak

I AM A TOURIST

Hisham Awad makes sure to see Bourj Hammoud and Karantina through colorless glasses (in other words, the ethical way).

LOYALLY PHOTOGRAPHING BOURJ HAMMOUD'S BRIDGE

Uncharted territories, ranging from a land ravaged by war, to an interior with intimate stories to tell, should always be seen with new eyes. However, historical discoveries of new lands and rediscoveries of deserted lands have repeatedly proven that it's impossible to gain genuinely new perceptions. After all, colonial eyes are also nostalgic eyes, and are only capable of looking at these territories in a way that belongs to other spaces and different times. Regardless of whether the discoveries are grand – be it the discovery of the New World, or a small unexpected encounter, like an alley in Beirut – one has to create alternative ways to view a space because every space sets its own rules. These rules are not flexible, nor can they be ignored. Places like Bourj Hammoud, specifically the region under the colossal bridge, redefine relationships that may have previously seemed trivial, the most significant being that of light and shadow.

It is not an option to return home with nice photographs taken under Bourj Hammoud's bridge, at least not an ethical option. If the ethical tourist wishes to loyally illustrate the uncompromising bridge he or she must abandon all quests for aestheticism. Proper lighting should be the least of your worries, since sufficient light at the actual Bourj Hammoud space was never part of the bridge's priority either.

As soon as you enter Bourj Hammoud, it becomes clear that the neighborhood is like no other. It is big and functional enough to be independent of adjacent spaces. Yet inevitably you are reminded that it is only a sub-space, a sub-entity. The neighborhood is hidden and physically bound by concrete layers that separate two very different views of the city. Considering the bridge. There is the view from above the bridge, the mute highway to Achrafieh, that seems eager to deny the existence of the

Photo by George Zouein

neighborhood, and there is a view from underneath the bridge that immediately exposes the residential and social aspects of the neighborhood. Standing underneath the bridge it is clear that Bourj Hammoud has minimal architectural ambitions. There is, for instance, no public space as such. Underneath the bridge, with its well-defined concrete horizon, expectations are instantly set. Even in broad daylight there is more shade than light. Light penetrates through small divergences between sections of the bridge, gently hinting that the space is almost, but not yet, apocalyptic. Underneath the bridge, day resembles night.

GUIDE TO 'LOYALLY' PHOTOGRAPHING FROM UNDERNEATH THE BRIDGE

01. Stand at the side of the highway that takes you to Sin-El-Fil. You are facing the bridge.
Take out your camera and set your shutter speed to 160. Take a photograph.

02. Start walking under the bridge. Take a photograph at the same shutter speed and overall settings.

03. Keep going. Take another photograph.

04. Keep on taking photographs with the same shutter speed, regardless of the light.
You will notice that your photos will sometimes be well exposed, sometimes not. Sometimes they will be completely dark. You should forget planning your aesthetics, since the space underneath the Bourj Hammoud Bridge is probably the only street where light is constantly changing. There are parts where the bridge touches the buildings on the side and everything is shaded. And there are parts where daylight comes through. During the night, the bridge politely disappears into the street.

PARTICIPATING IN THE IMAGINED INAUGURATION OF THE TRANSFERRED ARMENIAN MONUMENT

As you are walking through the shadows cast by the concrete, you will notice groups of people, all heading in the same direction. Follow them. As the groups start to grow and the individual walks faster, your curiosity will be rekindled. They are all dressed up, their faces brimming with joy. They are impatient. All gets clearer the moment the traffic becomes overwhelming and the chatter between the citizens is excessive. You can feel the hype, even through the unintelligible Armenian words.

There it is, the reason for all the commotion: a block of iron, in the middle of the Bourj Hammoud central square. The nearby shops are closed. Everyone, including the kids and the elderly, is witnessing the transfer of one of the most important Armenian monuments to the martyrs of the massacre.

The unveiling of the base of the monument (an iron monolith) has been a hot topic of conversation for a month or so here in Bourj Hammoud. That which has long been present in Bourj Hammoud , at least in the form of a printed image on the calendars of the local political parties, began to occupy three dimensions when, for the entire hour of the inauguration, time became stretched in two directions: seventy-five years back into the Armenian past (to 1915 and the onset of the Armenian Genocide) and one hour forward into the Lebanese present.

DRINKING JERMUK: ARMENIAN SPARKLING WATER

The festive inauguration was hot (almost thirty-five celcius degrees in the shade) and tiring. For the dehydrated Bourj Hammoud offered Armenian sparkling water called 'Jermuk'. Jermuk is of a quality rivalling the best known of French and American brands, though it is exclusive to the Middle East, of course.

Jermuk, the brand name of the water, is the name of a city in the southern Armenian province of Vayots Dzor. Actually, if a visitor looked closely at the names of streets and shops in Bourj Hammoud, they may notice that many represent an Armenian region, city, mountain or river, such as Arax Street, which is originally the name of a river that runs through present day Turkey, Armenia, Iran and Azerbaijan. Bourj Hammoud is a sort of Lebanese equivalent to the Chinatowns of the Western world.

To find oneself drinking a bottle of Armenian sparkling water in a café in the center of Bourj Hammoud, which is situated next to an oversized representation of a Coca Cola bottle, is not an likely everyday occurrence. This eclecticism is the reason why so many are drawn to the area.

As you walk to a grocery store, Armenian posters will cover the walls and you hear Armenian being spoken by many around you. So, Bourj Hammoud lives in permanent conflict, it is a desired mutation of Armenia, but with all the problems particular to Beirut: power cuts, water shortages, scarce parking space. This duality destroys Bourj Hammoud's illusion of an alternative Armenia, but it does separate it from other neighborhoods in Beirut. As a tourist you will take notice.

KARANTINA: FALSE THRESHOLDS AND IMPLICIT WARNINGS

Wandering around Karantina is an assault on the senses, due to the fact that there are too many sources, all contradictory. One should look but not listen, or listen but not look. The misery is obvious, yet the inhabitants deny it. One can roam through an industrial area, followed by a residential zone in less than five minutes. The unsubtle shift is radical, unethical. The industrial zone gives warning of what lies ahead, when you see the robust façades of the factories you also hear the voices of children playing and the voices of street vendors.

The contrast is unsettling. The Karantina district desperately wants (but fails) to create a utopia of urban planning, since the highway separates the 'producing' from the 'using' area. The highway is a neutralizing element, since passers-by (drivers and pedestrians) can have no grasp on how the Karantina functions at its two extremes. Few people know that behind the flour and metal factories lies a slum where the puddles of water on the roads reflect crumbling façades. Even I did not know, until very recently.

I am a tourist in my own country.

> **Yes, you will come back
> with dark prints,
> overexposed ones, abstractions
> of space and experience.
> It is 'ethical', nonetheless.**

Photos by Georges Zouein

Photos by George Zouein

50

FANTASY HOUSES

An invitation to engage in creative urban speculation.

A random stroll through one of the inner city areas – for example Manara, Gemayzeh, Ashrafieh, Bourj Hammoud or Hamra – is a possibility for some creative real estate speculation. Bring a pencil, some paper and do not forget your imagination.

The empty spaces and abandoned buildings in these neighborhoods are inspiring to the urban wanderer, as they form a potential opportunity to rethink the future of this piece of the built up environment. A lot of valuable real estate is in a state of decay in Beirut, since who owns it is often unclear. Yet these buildings capture many memories of the city's past.

A fantasy about a house or plot could be the starting point for a new, realistic development plan. Therefore, we invite you to visit the buildings listed here and redesign them, or perhaps another, to your liking. And as such, create incentives for owners, investors and developers to renovate, conserve and transform these buildings.

HOUSE – A (1930S) – LOWER SASSINE STREET

This mansion in Ashrafieh looks like a French army garrison. On the third floor of the building there are two separate rooms with a large flat roof in between. It has a beautiful façade and a quiet garden with a lot of shade afforded by huge fruit trees. In the garden there is another separate structure.

SPECULATION 1: TEUTONIC HOSTEL

We propose the conversion of this building into a type of hostel the city of Beirut has never seen before. A fantasy hostel combining the services of

top star hotels with facilities suitable to the expectations of low budget travelers. An improbable place where Sarah Palin meets Zaphod Beeblebrox – this new concept was born in Berlin following the fall of the Berlin Wall and the subsequent emergence of new trendy Teutonic city subculture. Posh people would stay here because they like luxury for cheap prices. They also want to be like the 'common' people, whom they do not understand. A hostel as a reality check.

HOUSE - B (1890S) - RUE MAR MIKHAIL
The building looks like a Florentine/Venetian palace. It has three floors and sea view from the front balcony. Since plans were announced for a highway, the building has been silently awaiting its demolition.

SPECULATION 2: PALAZZO FOR THE ARTS
This palazzo is a perfect place to start a journey in Beirut – if your aim is to decipher the myth of the Beiruti Casanovas, who gather here for a close encounter with the arty and slightly upper class bohemian community. This community is the reason Beirut has a different pulse to the rest of the Middle East – if it wasn't for those freaks this city would be like any Arab city. If you're into watching pony-tailed armpits performing weird shows in improvised glass boxes or highly eclectic, minimalist, oriental electronics, or pseudo intellectual fake blonds wearing rompers discussing the weather on Jupiter's ring, this is the place for you.

I remember a girl so very well
The carnival drums all mad in the air
Grim reapers and skeletons and a missionary bell
O where do we go now but nowhere

In a colonial hotel we fucked up the sun
And then we fucked it down again
Well the sun comes up and the sun goes down
Going round and round to nowhere

The kitten that padded and purred on my lap
Now swipes at my face with the paw of a bear
I turn the other cheek and you lay into that
O where do we go now but nowhere

O wake up, my love, my lover wake up
O wake up, my love, my lover wake up

Nick Cave

Fragment of 'Where do we go now but nowhere'

HOUSE - C (1920S) - RUE PASTEUR

This uncommon house, with its uncommon façade, occupies a strategic plot overlooking Rue Pasteur and the sea, whilst sitting dangerously close to the bustling and crowded Rue Gouraud. It is a real small palazzo, with its two floors and an external stone staircase. The garden is known for a surprising lime tree and goldfish tank. The building was constructed during the Ottoman period of Beirut.

SPECULTION 3: OTTOMAN BOUTIQUE

This place is about escapism, it is the place of the lime tree arbor where you go to escape the daily routine and where time almost stands still. So, you are sitting on the rooftop of the Institut du Monde Arabe in Paris, Armani suited, watching the stock market plummet on the screen of your laptop, and suddenly the music goes:

The official city is often recognizable from decorated buildings, monumental public squares, or statues representing political or economic power. Yet, in the case of Beirut, the official representation of the city is most clear at its limits. In those places where history, ideology, planning and commerciality are contested or simply ignored one gets a hint of what official vs. unofficial means. Perhaps due to the colonization, the destruction of the Civil War, or maybe because of all the different languages and alphabets, understanding a system of urban hierarchy feels like a slippery slope. Each time we think we've got it, our feeling of center and periphery is challenged, a back alley road is officially blocked off, a piece of coast appropriated or a poster celebrates another political alliance.

 Old Townhouses in Ownership Limbo

BUILDINGS

 The Bullet-ridden Martyr Square Statue

MONUMENTS

 The Downtown Disneyland

PLANNING

 The Abandoned Train Station

INFRASTRUCTURE

 Service Taxi System

TRADE + SERVICES

Photo by Jeannette Gaussi

OFFICIAL
CITY

Mona Harb

STORY OF A NAME

Al-Dahiya is a label designating the southern neighborhoods of Beirut and associated with a set of representations related to Shia groups, Hezbollah's domination, poverty, anarchy and illegality. Al-Dahiya is also an Arabic term signifying 'the suburb'.

The name delineates a specific geographic territory which extends south of the capital city over an area equal to that of municipal Beirut, housing half a million residents. Thus, al-Dahiya is a name that homogeneizes a myriad of neighborhoods with different social, economic and urban histories into one whole perceived as a distinct other. How did al-Dahiya became the stigmatizing label of the southern neighborhoods of Beirut? This essay attempts to tell the brief story of al-Dahiya's name.

The naming of the surrounding neighborhoods of Beirut into the term 'suburb' or 'periphery' begins in the 1930s with reports of foreign urban sociologists and urban planners who are seeking to diagnose the ills of the city and determine policies to improve its functioning (René Danger, Michel Ecochard). These planning studies propose new towns for the suburbs which would attract the middle-classes out of the city center and allow for a planned, rational and hygienic urban growth. In the 1960s and 1970s, using French models prevailing at the time, analysis highlights the growth of the city from its center

towards its suburbs ('banlieues') according to concentric rings that formed misery belts (Bourgey and Pharès 1973). This analysis is actually disconnected from the reality of the urban structure that was organized instead along linear axis of circulation linking the north-eastern and southern neighborhoods to its city center since the late nineteenth century, and within which Palestinian camps and informal settlements developed as of the early 1950s.

The 'misery belt' and 'suburbs' lexicon is recuperated by a range of public and private institutions, as well as by researchers and journalists who all disseminate the concept and its associated representations. At the time, the label concerns all the suburbs of Beirut (al-dawahi) that are described as poor, rural, chaotic and illegal. The suburbs are differentiated between their northern (shamaliyya) and southern (janubiyya) parts. They are still not directly associated with a predominant confessional group as both include Maronite and Shia populations. The mobilization of the leftist groups in the late 1960s and their progressive focus around the Shia constituency led by Imam Moussa al-Sadr starts the territorialization process of the suburbs, i.e. the association of the space with a political identity. The suburbs become the space of the oppressed, the disenfranchised and the marginalized. Rapidly, with the start of the Civil War in 1974, this association takes up a sectarian dimension and becomes specifically Shia. The southern suburbs of Beirut become a Shia territory, protected by the Amal movement[1] militia.

1   The Amal movement is the acronym of 'Afwaj al-muqawama al-lubnaniyya 'which is the armed wing of the Movement of the Dispossessed ('Harakit al-Mahroumin') established by Imam Moussa al-Sadr. For more on the movement, see A.R. Norton, *Amal and the Shia: Struggle for the Soul of Lebanon*, Austin: Un. Of Texas Press, 1987.

The forced displacement of Shia groups from the northern sections of Beirut in the mid-1970s and from the Southern towns of Lebanon after the Israeli invasion of 1978 consolidates the now dominant Shia demography in the southern parts of the capital. In the early 1980s, the increased violence on Maronites living in the southern suburbs pushes them to leave their lands and homes towards the northern sections of Beirut. The division of the city into territorial enclaves is achieved during these early years, through similar processes of population displacement in other neighborhoods.

In the early 1980s, al-Dahiya al-janubiyya (the southern suburb) becomes the term used to label the area extending south of the capital towards the airport. Progressively, the suffix al-janubiyya is abandoned and 'al-Dahiya' becomes the term used to refer to this section of Beirut: everyone knows where 'the suburb' is and, most importantly whose suburb it is. Al-Dahiya is equated with a Shia ghetto, a rebel territory, a place where rural migrants, not accustomed to urbanity and prone to religious fundamentalism, live in an anarchic and miserable environment, outside any State control. In 1982, shortly after the Israeli invasion of Beirut, under the presidency of Amin Gemayel, the public agents attempt to restore their authority over the suburbs and destroy 400 illegal dwellings in Ouzai: the intervention ends in violent confrontations with the residents and Amal militia which yield several

deaths and wounded. The suburbs' perception of the state as the enemy is associated with this episode to this day. In 1984, the Beirut's intifada leads to the division of the Army and the domination of the Amal movement over the city and its suburbs, alongside other allied militias. Daily urban governance becomes managed and controlled by these armed groups who parasite the state's institutions, tax the residents, and redistribute their resources to their clienteles[2].

2   For a detailed analysis of the urban economics of the militias during the Lebanese Civil War, see E. Picard, *The Demobilization of the Lebanese Militias*, Oxford: Center for Lebanese Studies, 1999.

In 1984, Hezbollah declares its existence as a military Islamic resistance against the Israeli occupation. In parallel to its military training, the party deploys its network of social institutions in the key Shia areas of Lebanon: the Beqaa, the South and al-Dahiya. Schools, clinics, mosques and husseyniyyat, kindergartens, water tanks, electric generators, etc. are carefully distributed in neighborhoods of villages and towns, providing professional services to needy residents at very cheap prices[3]. Progressively, the constituency of Hezbollah grows and feeds into this institutional network, rendering it more grounded in the socio-spatial structure. A major interruption halts this evolution before accelerating it further: the

3   More information on the institutional networks of Hezbollah can be found in M. Harb, *Le Hezbollah: de la banlieue à la ville*, Paris et Beyrouth: Karthala et IFPO, forthcoming and M. Harb & R. Leenders, 'Know Thou Enemy: Hizballah and the Politics of Perception', *Third World Quarterly* no. 26(1), 2005, pp. 73-197.

growth of Hezbollah is not well regarded by Amal that sees the party as a threat to its power base. Frictions begin as of 1987 in relation to the war of the Palestinian camps which oppose Amal militia to Fatah in al-Dahiya. They degenerate in 1989 when military clashes oppose Amal movement to Hezbollah's armed men in the streets of the southern suburbs. The party of God quickly eradicates Amal and confines it to the edges of al-Dahiya. The military standoff is consecrated by a Syrian-Iranian deal which forces both armed groups to restrain to specific territories: Hezbollah dominates the

Beqaa, Amal rules in the South while al-Dahiya's is under the jurisdiction of both, though Hezbollah's gets the lion's share of its neighborhoods and Amal stays in its peripheries [4].

4   A detailed account of these events is available in R. Sayigh, *Too Many Enemies. The Palestinian Experience in Lebanon*, London: Zed Books, 1994.

As of 1989, al-Dahiya becomes managed by Hezbollah's governing apparatus. The end of the Civil War in 1990 prompts the party to revise its political strategy vis-à-vis its existence within a consociative system of governance. In 1992, after two years of internal negotiations, Hezbollah decides to participate to the Lebanese political system and runs for parliamentary elections. This is the start of what has been termed its 'lebanonization' process [5]. The party

5   See N. Hamzeh, 'Lebanon's Hizbullah: From Islamic Revolution to Parliamentary Accommodation', *Third World Quarterly* no.14(2), 1993, pp. 321-337.

abandons parts of its revolutionary ideals and joins the power-sharing game that defines the Lebanese quagmire. This choice impacts its spatial and territorial inscribing which progressively tolerates more socio-cultural variations, though it does not challenge the party's domination. Hence, as of the mid-1990s, we carefully notice a partial conversion of the meanings associated with al-Dahiya's label. The re-entry of the State in the suburbs through a set of reconstruction and reform projects is largely associated with this change: public institutions (schools, dispensaries, hospitals...) are re-instated, highways and roads are built; in 1998, municipal elections are held. Indeed, the capital city is seeking to modernize its peripheries, with the declared aim of better administration and organization – which also implies improved monitoring and control.

Other economic elements contribute to this cognitive conversion: the early 1990s were times of economic boom in Lebanon, bringing large amounts of transnational capital into the city, benefiting all parties who agreed to respect each other's turf and not meddle into each other's transactions – this consensus was referred to as the 'troïka',

The suburbs become the space of the oppressed, the disenfranchised and the marginalized. Rapidly, with the start of the Civil War in 1974, this association takes up a sectarian dimension and becomes specifically Shia.

in reference to the three poles of power ruling the political system: the Sunnis, the Shia and the Maronites [6]. Thus, while Hariri was reconstructing downtown Beirut using Gulf-based capital, Hezbollah was consolidating its military resistance in the South and simultaneously attending to its constituency's service needs through its network of institutions centered in al-Dahiya, using Iranian and Shia diaspora capital. And, while Hezbollah would facilitate the evacuation of Shia squatters from downtown Beirut (negotiating on their behalf handful compensations), and its deputies wouldn't oppose the creation of the real-estate company in Parliament, Hariri would privilege a laisser-faire attitude vis-a-vis the production of what Hezbollah termed its 'Resistance society' in Dahiya.

6   On the troika, refer to J. Bahout, 'Deux ans après les elections legislatives de l'été 1992, où en le parlementarisme libanais ?', *Relations internationales et stratégiques* no. 16, 1994, pp. 57-66.

These tacit cooperations certainly did not exclude antagonisms especially when parties' interests intersected spatially. In the mid-1990s, a planning project is designed by the office of Hariri for the western section of the southern suburb, seeking to liberate the coast from all illegal settlements and develop its neighborhoods according to the standards of urban modernity. The project, called Elyssar (ironically, the queen of the Phoenician city Carthage) was contested by Hezbollah and Amal, not in relation to its planning approach and values, but in relation to its institutional setup which excluded them. Negotiations insured that they ultimately altered the structure of the project into a public agency where their representatives joined the board of administration. Thus, Hezbollah, Amal and Hariri became partners in re-planning the southern peripheries into a modern city, freed from its poverty and illegality, and up to the level of the capital city Hariri was eager to produce and sell to its network of developers [7].

During those post-war reconstruction years, al-Dahiya becomes the subject of a more varied set of representations, depending on one's positionality

> Thus, while Hariri was reconstructing downtown Beirut using Gulf-based capital, Hezbollah was consolidating its military resistance in the South and simultaneously attending to its constituency's service needs through its network of institutions centered in al-Dahiya, using Iranian and Shia diaspora capital.

7   A more detailed analysis of
Elyssar's urban governance is found
in M. Harb, 'Urban Governance
in Post-War Beirut: Resources,
Negotiations, and Contestations
in the Elyssar Project'. In S. Shami
(ed.), *Capital Cities: Ethnographies
of Urban Governance in the Middle
East*, Toronto: Toronto University
Press, 2001, pp.111-133.

in the city and its soci-
ety. For some, it evokes
fearful associations with
'Hezbollah land' or
'Dahiyat al-Khomeyni':
its boundaries are well
perceived and carefully
avoided. For Hezbollah's
constituency, it is a label of which they are proud
as it symbolizes their steadfastness and determi-
nation. For the public administration, the label has
been recuperated and is now used as a geographic
destination on the highway signposts. For planners
and development agencies, al-Dahiya is in need
of dire planning and organizing – a site of experi-
mentation for their social and urban agendas. For
others, the southern suburbs are just a part of the
city, a geographical reference to the place you tell
the cab to drive, a destination which sells 'cheaper'
stuff than the city, a place where they can find af-
fordable food, clothing, furniture and other services. This is perhaps the time when al-Dahiya is
the most favorable to socio-spatial appropriations
by a multiplicity of users – though its political domination by Hezbollah is not challenged.

However, with the geopolitical changes that follow
the assassination of Rafik Hariri in February 2005,
and fifteen of his close collaborators in repeated
car explosions in following months, the relationship between Beirut and al-Dahiya quickly returns
to its violent behavior. The hostility is further fueled
by the Israeli War on Lebanon in July 2006. The
variety of representations about al-Dahiya is rapidly reduced to the binary reading that prevailed
during the Civil War years: al-Dahiya returns to
be Hezbollah's territory which rebels against the
righteous city – associated with Hariri's city. His
advocates – the 'March 14 camp' – claim 'Beirut is
a red line',and 'Beirut is ours'. Yet Hezbollah, one
of the main leaders of the opposition group – 'the
March 8 camp' – labels Dahiya: 'the rebel that
never dies', and the 'territory of the proud and the
glorious'. In winter 2007, the opposition organizes

a sit-in in downtown Beirut requesting the resig-
nation of the Lebanese government. The 'tent city'
paralyzes all economic life in Solidere's territory
for more than a year. Beirutis call it an 'invasion of
their city'. Opinion pieces in newspapers reject the
rural migrants that are 'ruralizing' Beirut, and deso-
late over the transformation of the beautiful neat
streets of downtown into a 'Dahiya landscape'. The
peripheries are accused of having robbed the city
of its modernity and civilization. Rare are the voices
praising the public life that has come to enliven the
sanitized spaces of downtown. The paroxysm of
this dichotomy is reached in May 2008 when, in
response to Hariri's attempts to clamp down on
Hezbollah's communication networks, the opposition enters Beirut and raids Hariri's offices, leading
to injuries, deaths and the take-over of the city by
the opposition, albeit for a few days. The fear of
the city from its rebel peripheries which grew as a
monster at its doorstep is physically materialized.

A year later, at the time of writing this essay, in
June 2009, the Lebanese parliamentary elections have taken place peacefully and both op-
ponent camps are now renegotiating the terms of
their participation to the next government in what
very likely seems another round of power-sharing
benefiting the already enriched merchant elites at
the expense of their constituencies. The city with
its suburbs will undoubtedly be the site of both
groups' ambitions for real-estate speculation dis-
guised within the narrative of economic development and tourism. The city-suburbs dichotomy will
hence probably be partially diluted into renewed
representations, as the 1990s period already witnessed, but again, only for a short term, as we await
the next cycle of visible violence.

Photo by Jeannette Gaussi

INTRA MUROS CITY TOUR

We are going to have a tour in Beirut's historic center. The old city practically remained unchanged from the end of the Byzantine Empire until the end of the eighteenth - beginning of the nineteenth - century. The tour will take place in what was the intra muros city (the city within the walls), and we are starting here precisely because we are standing next to what used to be one of the city gates, the one closest to the port.

01. The road that you see here, going through the old gate, traversing the old center and leading to the region of Saifi used to be one of the main Roman axial streets, the Decumanus Maximus. Later on we will visit the second Roman axis, the Cardo Maximus.

In that hole in the ground you can see some ruins. These are probably what remains of a caravanserai, a place for the merchants to rest, eat and sleep, conveniently placed next to the city gate. Note the ground level of the building, and note the actual ground level now; the old ground level is significantly lower, almost two stories lower, which gives you an idea of the amount of construction work that took place here.

If you look closely at those remains, you'll be able to tell that they date back to the Roman or Byzantine period. It was not unusual for builders to 'recycle' stones, so to speak, from older buildings and use them in newer ones.

If you look in that direction you can see the sea and the port of Beirut; the sea was much closer then. The port of Beirut became important in the eighteenth century because of the growing trade. The main export was a highly valued white silk produced in the mountains that you can see in the background, transported to Beirut and then shipped to the rest of the world. The accumulation of capital and money which ensued from that trade, is one of the reasons for the modernity that started in Beirut at the end of the eighteenth century.

The old city of Beirut numbered around 8000 inhabitants, 5000 of them were Sunni Muslims, 2000 Greek Orthodox and Melkites, and the rest were divided between minorities of Greeks, Jews, Armenians, Italians, Copts, etc. Basically people from all around the Mediterranean who came to the booming city, and those people, like all minorities in all cities, lived always close to the port because they usually worked in trade.

So when the walls fell in the 1840, after they were bombarded from the sea by the British fleet because of the war between the Egyptian Wali Mohammed Ali (backed by the French) and the Ottoman Empire (backed by the British), they were never rebuilt, because the notion of a walled city became anachronistic when the city itself was in full expansion.

One of the first major arteries of expansion was the one you can see here, which links the city center through the old Roman road with Gemayzeh, leading to the hill of Ashrafieh. What's interesting is that, even though Beirut was really small, people used to consider their relatives living outside the wall, their sons and daughters probably, as living abroad (*bil ghirbeh*). This was their world, their whole universe, and when you left the old city you were considered to be in foreign lands.

02. To your left is the Omari mosque, and the Beirut City Hall is to your right. Contrary to what you might think (somebody just said 'it looks like Disneyland'), the City Hall was built during the late Ottoman period; it is a monumental building, indeed to show authority, its eclectic architecture demonstrating the openness and the willingness to modernize which characterized that period of the Ottoman Empire. The yellow stone used in the building is particular to Beirut and is abundant in its constructions. The openings are a mixture of Ottoman, Moroccan, Andalusian and even Venetian-style. The nineteenth was the century of eclecticism *par excellence*, the builders here, for instance, even had catalogues with all types of openings, banisters, frames, and all the building elements they could choose from. If you were a builder in those times, all the styles of the world were available to you.

The Amir Assaf mosque, on the other hand, is one of Beirut's older mosques (built in 1523); like all the mosques and churches that we are going to see in the old city, it is quite modest in size. This is not Istanbul or Cairo, where mosques showed religious and political authority, the population here was very small and the city was on the edge of an empire, an insignificant, forgotten city for a long time. So all the places of worship are in keeping with the scale of the city, very small and integrated in the urban fabric. The fabric is now destroyed, but you can try and imagine this mosque as not being set apart like it is now but integrated with other buildings around it, with a very modest scale and architectural presence.

It was not unusual for builders to 'recycle' stones, so to speak, from older buildings and use them in newer ones.

The other mosque there (the Omari mosque) looks like a church because it was actually a Byzantine church, which was converted into a mosque after the Islamic conquest of the city (635 AD), and it later became the cathedral of St. John under the Crusaders (legend says that part of the remains of Saint John the Baptist, the prophet Yihya in Islam, are kept in the mosque to this day). It was re-transformed into a mosque after the Mamelukes took Beirut back from the Crusaders.

03. We can stop here and talk a bit about the early twentieth century architecture that you can see around you. Most of these houses have recently been restored, but what's interesting, besides their architectural characteristics, is the relationship they establish with what was then the new public space: the street. The old city, before modernization, was largely composed of small alleys (*zawarib*, dead-end streets). These *zawarib* were occupied mainly by people of the same family; they would start with very narrow openings that widened into courtyards in order to dissuade strangers, or non-family members, from entering. The inner courts constituted a shared space for the families, or more precisely for members of the same extended family; these shared spaces are

INTRA MUROS CITY MAP

a. Martyrs Square
b. Old Khan Ruins
c. Amir Assaf Mosque
d. Beirut Municipality Building
e. Al Omari Mosque
f. St Elie Church
g. St Georges Church
h. Maarad Street
i. Grand Theatre
j. Riad El Solh Square
k. Armenian Church
l. Ottoman Barracks,
    Government Headquarters
m. Roman Baths
n. Parliament Building
o. Place de l'Etoile

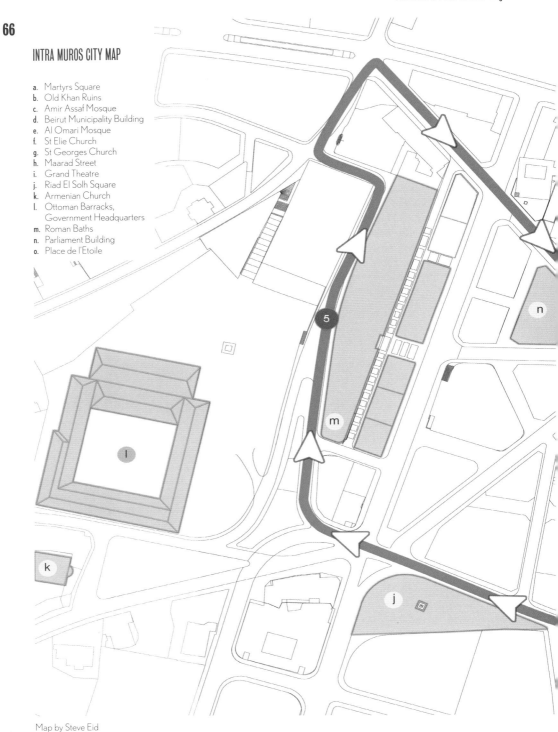

Map by Steve Eid

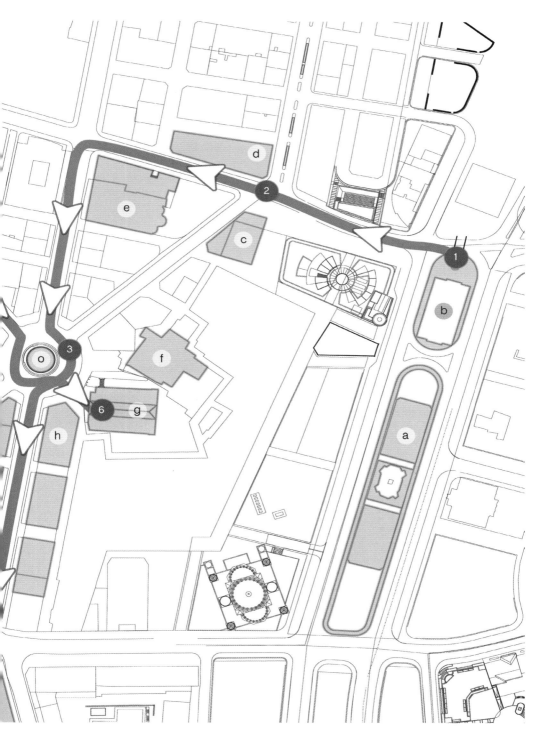

not exactly what we understand today as public space – they were obviously not meant to be public, and they are not absolutely private domains either. The duality of spaces that we are so accustomed to today (between public and private, inner and outer, domestic and political, etc.) was not in effect these days. People understood their city differently, and those who lived in it, had a complete mental map of all these shared domains – which is a vision radically different from what the early Orientalists described as cities made up of mazes and labyrinths.

The façade became a separation, like a skin, distinguishing what is interior from what is exterior, the private from the public, the subjective from the objective.

Actually there were no mazes, but spaces which were extremely structured, and in that sense we have to understand the logic of what has been termed 'introverted spaces'.

If we jump back to the beginning of the twentieth century and look at the façade of that building, we will notice that people were starting to be aware that something new was taking shape. Imagine this street, not filled with cars as it is now, but with merchants and passersby coming and going, the hustle and bustle of it all. The new wide streets became the new public space that people had to interact with. Contrary to the façades of the buildings defining the zawaribs with their narrow or sometimes absent openings, the façades of the new buildings are much more opened, and the façade became a separation, like a skin, distinguishing what is interior from what is exterior, the private from the public, the subjective from the objective, the domestic from the political space of the street. All these dualities, which started in the Renaissance, appeared here with modernization.

New liberties were found and people who came here at the end of the nineteenth century and the beginning of the twentieth would talk about Beirut as 'the city which smelled like freedom'.

We will now take the other Roman main road, the Cardo Maximus, which means that the old Roman Forum used to be somewhere where we're standing now.

If you look between those buildings, you can see the sea, and a bit further east is where the old port used to be, with a huge chain between two towers to lock the port at night and to prevent enemy ships from coming in. What's interesting is that this chain is a rather new addition, dating from Ottoman times. This points to a dilemma that is still shaping the spaces of Beirut to this day: in the Phoenician or Roman or Byzantine periods, Beirut was in the heart of large empires with the Mediterranean Sea in their heart, while in Arab times it was on the outer periphery of an empire which was largely oriented towards the inner regions. The Roman or Byzantine city did not need to defend itself from the sea, while the Arab and Ottoman city needed those defenses. So the dilemma can be summarized as follows: Is Beirut looking towards the sea and turning its face away from the mountains and the lands beyond them, or is it looking inwards towards the mountains and turning its back to the sea? I imagine this dilemma shaped the rather recent debate about opening Martyrs' Square to the sea or giving it the shape and the morphology of a closed square like those found in old Arab cities.

We're standing now in the Place de l'Etoile, the heart of the French Mandate Beirut. The area is actually quite well preserved, and as you might have noticed, the urban fabric of the French Mandate period is the only one that remains today; the Ottoman city has been completely destroyed – and ironically this began in the late Ottoman period, with the beginnings of modernization.

The Place de l'Etoile is a replica of a lot of star-shaped squares found in Paris. It has the shape of a star, a circle with eight spokes or radiuses emanating from it. The French authorities destroyed a large chunk of the older Ottoman city (or what then remained of it) in order to construct a symbol for their political and cultural powers: the parliament building, its library, the clock tower in the middle of the square to standardize time, so to speak, the Maarad Street (Exhibition Street), etc.

Before we take Maarad Street, you can see that if you count the spokes of the star there are only six. The reason for that is the two churches over there, the Church of Saint George for the Greek Orthodox and St Elie Church for the Greek Melkites. The French, who posited themselves as the protectors of the Christians in the Orient, could not destroy the churches of those whom they claimed they were protecting, and even though Baron Haussmann practically destroyed all the fabric of Paris without any consideration for religious buildings, the French couldn't do the same here.
A modernity cut short by the physical presence of two churches.

Maarad Street is one of the main urban interventions of the French Mandate period. Notice the pedestrian walkways, the covered galleries and the wide sidewalks. Notice also the attention to details and the addition of balconies to the façades. The concept of a balcony was new at the time, and it can only be justified by the fact that there was something to see outside, that there was an 'outside', which was the new public space of the street, to begin with. The notion of the street as a public space, or the space where modernity unfolds itself, is very present in nineteenth century European and American literature, from Charles Baudelaire to Edgar Allan Poe and E.T.A. Hoffmann.

We started on the eastern wall and now we are where the southern wall used to be.
We will walk along the wall until we reach the Roman baths and then we turn and come back here. Note that the Roman baths are actually

outside the walls of the medieval city, which means that the Roman city was significantly larger than the Ottoman one.

04. The building in renovation in front of you is Le Grand Théâtre; the area next to it there in the distance is what used to be the red light district of Beirut. Prostitutes would not stand in 'vitrines' (display windows) like in Amsterdam, but on the landings of the wide staircases of the old buildings (which are now practically all destroyed). These staircases were opened to the street, and they constituted a buffer zone between public and private spaces. The concept was not limited to that zone, but you can actually still find some of these buildings and their peculiar staircases all around Beirut – the buffer zone would be used by the inhabitants of the building, especially women, to negotiate, for instance with street vendors and ambulant salesmen.

The street which is ahead of us is the Rue des Banques (Banks' Street) which used to be the banking district, and one of the places that remained relatively undamaged and operational during the wars of 1975 to 1990, even though it is positioned at the heart of the infamous 'Green Line' that used to separate East Beirut from West Beirut. Its buildings are a good example of International Style 1950's architecture.

The small hill that you can see there used to be the limit of the old city wall. In the late Ottoman period, the Ottomans built a large barracks, strategically positioned, and it was later transformed into the headquarters of the government. An additional floor was added to the building when it was renovated in the 1990s, changing its scale and upsetting its original proportions.

05. These are the remains of the Roman baths, which are of course quite an interesting tourist attraction, but what I like most about this place is this lonely olive tree there, bursting out of the white rock. I cannot stress enough

Photo by Jeannette Gaussi

72

the importance of olive trees in this part of the world, because at some point in time, even nowadays in some regions, they meant the difference between life and death for the people who planted and cared for them. Actually an olive tree is compared to a boy... it will start bearing fruit fifteen years after being planted, the age when the boy becomes a man, and from its fruit is extracted the precious liquid, the oil that was used to anoint the kings of long-gone periods... the same oil that was used to anoint Jesus Christ, 'Christ' coming from the Greek word Xristos, which means 'the anointed one', or Massih in Arabic and Mshiho in Aramaic.

As we walk back to the Place de l'Etoile along the Roman ruins, you can see how nothing of the old city remains. It has been replaced by modern buildings and future malls. The old souks of Beirut erased forever.

The tour is nearing its end.

06. We end it by visiting one of the two churches that I spoke of earlier, next to the Place de l'Etoile, the Greek Orthodox Church of St. Georges. St. Georges is considered to be the patron saint of Beirut, and the legend says that the battle between him and the dragon took place just outside the city. (In the Islamic tradition, St. Georges is usually associated with Al-Khodr).

The Greek Orthodox and the Greek Melkite churches are actually not 'Greek' per se, but both of them, as well as the Maronite church, belong to the Church of Antioch, which was the first church founded by Saint Peter and Saint Paul after leaving Jerusalem for Rome. It was one of the four major churches of the old Christian world (the Church of Constantinople, the Church of Antioch, the Church of Jerusalem and the Church of Alexandria), and the only Church (congregation) in the world that has an uninterrupted record of its patriarchs dating back to Saint Peter.

Let's go inside.

As you can see, both the architecture of the Byzantine churches and the icons which are all around us, presents the visitor with a notion of space which is radically different from the 'modern' space created during the European Renaissance; let's say that it's a space that is illuminated from within, a space where the dualities of inside and outside, of subjective and objective, etc., are replaced with a distinction between what is from this world and what is not. The perspective paintings of the Renaissance invite their viewers to penetrate them with their gaze, to 'forget' the surface on which they are painted, while the Byzantine icons display their surface to the viewer as an insurmountable barrier, the barrier that separated the sacred from the profane, this world from the next... which is exactly reproduced architecturally by the iconostasis.

Here the notion of illuminated space is inscribed everywhere. And maybe it is the light of cities that ceased to exist physically, but still weigh heavily on our present.

Reem Saouma

ACCIDENTAL MONUMENTS

Monument to The Devastation of Downtown

Monument to Modernity

Beyroutes
City Center Cinema

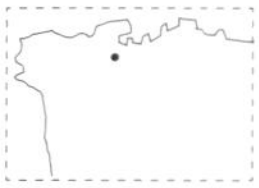

Accidental monuments

Monument to The Devastation of Downtown

Beyroutes
Charles Helou Station

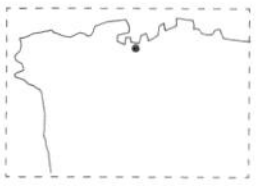

Accidental monuments

Monument to Modernity
The biggest public toilet in the Middle East

Monument to the Green Line

Monument to the War of the Hotels

Beyroutes
Barakat Building

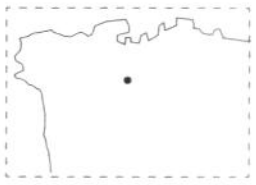

Accidental monuments

Monument to the Green Line
A sole survivor in a rapidly rebuilt city

Beyroutes
The Holiday In Hotel

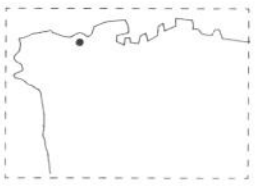

Accidental monuments

Monument to the War of the Hotels
Why do we need new towers when we still have empty old ones?

FROM AUH TO AUB
The Old, the Renovated and the Fake

The American University Hospital (AUH) is located northwest of Hamra Street, south of the Clemenceau neighborhood, east of Ein el Mreisé, and north of Bliss Street, the street next to the American University of Beirut. Its website says that its current building was established in 1970 and at the time was considered to be state-of-the-art.

Beginning with the AUH itself, its main building is white and U-shaped, and belongs to the Modernist school of architecture that continued to take Lebanon, and specifically Beirut, by storm at the time. Being modern had the positive connotations of being progressive, educated, rich, and yes, Western, and all of that, therefore, should have made sense for the Medical Center of the American University of Beirut.

Always ahead, AUH's recently renovated emergency room was not refurbished to remain stylistically faithful to its mother building, but has instead an ultra-modern façade, so to speak, where wood and matt steel are the dominant materials. The surface of the ring between the main building of the hospital and the ER is not tarred but clad with granite, another material very much in vogue in Beirut in 2000. One particular feature about the ring, which is pretty stunning, is that the outdoor waiting area, with its plants and benches, is not highlighted from the street-through elevation, which serves to remind the spectator that this, too, is a public area.

The AUH is well situated, in the sense that its neighborhood shares its upward, westward ambitions, if one were to read things architecturally. North of AUH, as I mentioned, is the Clemenceau neighborhood, whose landmark is the Gefinor Compound, which could have been build in Munich. Its architecture is minimalist, clean, geometric, and grid-like, and its palette is black and white – it even comes with its own minimalist lighting. One of the three Gefinor buildings houses the Lufthansa main office, as well as l'ébéniste, an exhibition of Scandinavian glass for sale at ridiculously high prices. The salesperson in l'ébéniste is a young Lebanese woman who's French pronunciation would make Émilie Simon blush.

Closer to AUH, the middle Gefinor building is L-shaped and includes Gruen Eatery, another pricey, Teutonic dessert restaurant whose name, again, is set in white over black and in a sans serif. Gruen Eatery has a beautiful minimalist décor but even better, it overlooks the open plaza created by the L-shape of the building in which it is situated. I, a resident of Beirut, do not know of an open public space as large in this city (apart from the coastline of course). Not that that this plaza is large, but Beirut is not a city of large open spaces. The Green Field in AUB and its recently founded Charles Hostler Center do offer such an experience, but only within a private, American institution. All this affirms the idea of large, open space as the experience of the other, and which in turn affirms the foreignness of the Gefinor Compound experience.

Going from the Gefinor Compound towards AUB's Medical Gate, one passes by a renovated building, seemingly from the 1930s, whose art deco walls and flutings are painted in a light salmon color. The sign identifies the building as Galerie Arcache (yes, with the Frenchie spelling), again in a bold sans serif, but in black over white this time. Interestingly enough, the Arabic name is set in two circles, where 'Galerie' and 'Arcache' are

---

Interestingly enough, the Arabic name is set in two circles, where 'Galerie' and 'Arcache' are calligraphic and fitting their respective circles. Arabic therefore reads as exotic ornament, French as the real thing.

---

calligraphic and fitting their respective circles. The Arabic therefore reads as exotic ornament, while the French reads as the real thing.

Galerie Arcache's building is a small one. It belongs to a different decade, and a different school of architecture. The building marks a rough end to the urbane Hamra neighborhood and a rough beginning to the maritime Ein el Mreisé neighborhood. The buildings in Ein el Mreisé, smaller and more picturesque, suggest that Hamra was either inhabited in a later point in time, or at the expense of some earlier dwellings, and I incline towards the former. This is because when I was still in secondary school an old native Beirutiti taught me English who narrated history from a witness' perspective. He once told us, 'You see those old houses where Blisshouse is? When I was your age, we used to think that the forest area beyond it was inhabited by jinn (demons).' The eerie forest area he talked about was the current AUH, of course.

The shift in mood continues with the Pierre Y. AbouKhater (Fahed) Building. I am typing the name down exactly as I copied it, for the metallic sign at its inner gate is the only indication of life within. The Fahed Building, and let's call it the Fahed Building for convenience sake, is across the street from the newly (2002) inaugurated St. Jude Children's Cancer Center, and a few meters from Galerie Arcache. Only God and Mr. AbouKhater know what goes on inside, but my guess is that it is another AUB-affiliated building, and that it, like other old AUB-affiliated buildings, was carefully renovated to preserve its dignified attire. Whenever a functional unit was added - not renovated - to the building, the material used was that slick matt metal that was invading the country. This sincerely marks the additions as additions and not as fake constituents of the original building. It is clear that the choice to maintain the historical styles of the Fahed Building and Galerie Arcache buildings was recent and deliberate. This shows that the patrons of architecture in this part of town have come to develop a taste for the historical. Something that I think owes itself to the Lebanese Civil War and, of course, the zeitgeist, but also because in recent decades Beirut witnessed the rise of other ultra-modern cities in the Arab world. It didn't take long before the city realized that it was not to her advantage to join the race for size and modernity, and that it was to her advantage to emphasize her history, which no one could take from her. Not that Beirut cannot lose her architectural history, for she can, but that no one can make new cities any older.

Not so much that Beirut cannot lose her architectural history, for she can, but that no one can make new cities any older.

All of this is not to say that the statements has changed with the changing of its carrier. I say this because all this stylistic wealth is found within one block that is as heterogeneous as one block can be; all four groups of buildings discussed are interested in marketing themselves as classy, progressive, and well off, yet in doing so take three totally different directions, which leaves us with the impression that the patrons of architecture in this area are aware that style is only the beginning of a building's statement.

One particular phenomenon that's on my mind, and that I had expected to discuss, was the trend of historicizing not renovated historical buildings that Lebanon witnessed during the 1990s. But the block that I studied seemed to have veered away from this phenomenon, which reaffirms the idea of authenticity as a key to finesse and posits modern architecture at the heart of Beirut's architectural history. During their restoration the Galerie Arcache building and the Fahed Building were left mostly to their original designs, So were the main AUH building and the entire Gefinor Compound, and rightly so, because these modernist buildings are part of our national heritage.

Photos by Tarek Moukaddem

...IAN

Wandering through Beirut you find a mixed Arabic and Latin alphabet, sprinkled throughout shop and city signs. Then suddenly, a third type of characters appears – it seems as if all the names end with ...ian. Could you have stumbled into Armenia proper? No, you're east of central Beirut, in flamboyant Bourj Hammoud. A maze of narrow streets filled with friendly Lebanese-Armenian people and their hot, spicy food – where a discovery hides at each corner.

Guide by Zinab Chahine

special cut out version!

How to Survive in
Dahiya

The ultimate guide to help you make it through the day on your visit to Dahiya.

Beer

ZOOM LENS EF-S 18-5

قـف
STOP
BEYOND THIS POINT!
no cameras
no alcohol
no PDA

Dahyeh is one hell of an extraordinary area. People unfamiliar with the area hear many stories and urban myths - some true some not. This mini guide book is here to set the record straight. So whether you just want to sit back and relax or if you prefer to cut this out and head on over to Dahiya for an adventurous day. . . enjoy!

First things first...
Iconic images

Become familar with these images becuase your going to see them everywhere in Dahiya.

Driving and traffic

Don't bother with turn signals, people will only assume you accidently put them on.

It is not necessary to go around a roundabout.

If stuck in a traffic, just honk until traffic starts moving.

One-way streets do not exist. Cars will always fit in the smallest streets going in either direction

There are no traffic lights, but I've seen a few currently being installed.

If someone is driving the wrong way down the street, just shut up, pull over, and let him pass, God knows what he has on him or to what party he is in!

Seeing five people on a scooter is totally normal even with a baby on board.

Seat belts are not an issue. Sure as hell the police won't fine you for it.

There are no pay-for-parking lots, its a dog-eat-dog world to get a parking spot.

If your car horn doesn't work, don't bother coming to Dahiya.

"Don't follow me, I'm engaged" and "Follow me if you want to die" are just two of many funny phrases you will see on the back windows of vans and buses.

Walking around

Keep your purse facing the opposite side of the street, or carry a purse that goes across your shoulders, because motorcycle purse snatchers are common.

Don't panic when you hear firearms, it just means the speech is over!

They say that Saint Terez is the new mono.

If you bring a camera into Dahiya, you're just asking for trouble.

Sidewalks are not for walking, they are for street vendors.

Have somebody with you that knows the area, otherwise you will be as lost as a whore in church.

Holding hands is okay, but please don't take the PDA (public display of affection) any further than this.

During Ashoura it looks as if everyone is gothic, but they are dressed head in toe in black to mourn the death of Imam Houssan (nephew of Prophet Mohammad (PBUH).

There are no movie theaters and no gardens in Dahiya.

You only see three main flags (Hizbollah, Amal, Lebanese) but during the World Cup you see flags from all over the world, especially Germany!

Electricty

Don't start to straighten your hair unless you know there is a full hour of electricity. Half straight, half curly isn't the coolest hair style!

Getting stranded in an elevator is totally normal, just hit the door hard until somebody hears you.

Keep your laptop fully charged because when electricity is out, the boredom begins.

Typically, electricity cuts out every four hours.

A common household phrase is "did you flip it up/down?" Referring to electricity switches.

A bite to eat

Don't eat at just any shawarma or sandwich shop, you don't know how it's stored and handled. When in doubt, go for the place that has a crowd because you know it has a good reputation.

Argileh is your breakfast, lunch, and dinner

Every block has saj, manoushe and a dekene (minimarket)

You can find a cheap rotisserie chicken anywhere, but I wouldn't recommend it. Go to Harkous Chicken.

For the best fruit cocktail go to Al Reda in Estrad Sayed Hadi. Darwish is famous for its icecream, located in Maamoura (Bourj) and very popular with the locals.

Cremino is a high class French patisserie. If you're feeling brave try the cactus fruit flavor (subear).

Have a big family to feed on a budget? Try Abu Ali's Foul and Hummos, located in Rweiss. On Saturday or Sunday be prepared to wait in a one hour line and don't forget tupperware.

Is your big family wanting dessert after hummos? Take them to Ikhlas Bakery, located on the Old Saida Road. for genafeh gibne (cheesey dessert), although there's never a place to park there, and no guarantee that you won't get cussed out for blocking the main road.

For a cozy comfortable place to chill, go to Cafeyet for amazing hot drinks and argile, located in Estrad Sayed Hadi, next to Harkous Chicken.

saj

fruit cocktail

hummos

sandwich duh!

Shopping

Almost anything you need to buy you can find at Karout, but beware, it's all cheap Chinese stuff

Most stores close at or before 8 pm, and Sunday everybody is usually closed...so shop early.

No need to go to the supermarket! There are tons of guys pushing carts. They have everything from fresh produce, toys, fish, collecting metal, shoes, kleenex, and nuts.

The only mall in Dahiya is the newly opened Beirut Mall. It's a great place for annoying teenages, secret lovers, and bored families with no electricity.

Beleh (secondhand items) is the best place for slightly used clothes and shoes. I've found some great vintage dresses there.

The Ghoubeiry main street is the place to go for car parts and salvage yards.

A typical inersection

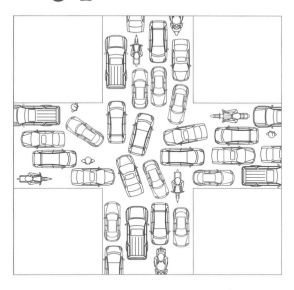

Watch out for:
scooters
pedestrians
beggers
cats
push carts

Don't forget to:
honk a lot
scream
curse
make hand gestures

How to get a good bargain

1. Don't look too interested in the product, this is a sign of weakness!

2. After asking his price, give your lowest price.

3. If he doesn't accept start to walk away (there is an 80% chance he will call you back).

4. Mention it is cheaper somewhere else, lie if you have to.

5. Show the product's weaknesses.

6. If he swears to Allah, his mother, and his seventh unborn child that he is losing money, don't believe him!

7. If you are a foreigner, disguise yourself and blend in as much as possible.

8. Open your wallet and show that all you have is X amount (hide the rest in your pocket if you have to).

Niels Lestrade

TRAFFIC POEM: SUPERFLUOUS THERAPY

See the crossroads in Beirut, how they
easily enclose,
under noisy honks and hoots, vehicles in
rising dose

See the random traffic lights, as a strife
for regulation,
and the uptight traffic knights, vainly
leading navigation

See how drivers better flow, and feel
clearly more at ease,
when police decide to go, and the traffic
lights all cease

Public proclaim end regulation, ordering
how traffic goes,
forms a pointless medication, when you
watch from very close

Edwin Gardner and Janneke Hulshof

CREATIVE MODERNISM

Come closer, the love is in the details.

Beirut is sprinkled with many pearls of modernism. Those who are willing to see can find them glimmering in the shadows. Those who look beyond the veil of dust, rust and scars can recognize the subtle elegance of Beirut's apartment buildings.

Details designed by human minds and made with human hands...

An elegant flavor of modernism is present everywhere in Beirut, neither dogmatic nor cutting edge. Beiruti modernism will not cut you, it will charm you. Where in the 1970s modernism in the West was being industrialized, in Beirut labor was still cheap. This allowed for elaborate concrete form work with sculptural balconies, welcoming canopies covering your path to the entrances that are secured with unique and artistic ironwork.

Train your eyes. Look close and you will find the love and passion with which the details of Beirut's breed of modernism were conceived.

Beirut is loved and hated, by its inhabitants, its diaspora and its foreign visitors. Beirut is also seductive and feared. The city's liberal character, its bars, restaurants and clubs have made of it the Paris of the Middle East. The East-West divide, the recent car bombs and street fights left scars on bodies and psyches, in families and in the city's architecture. Beirut, the emotional city, is the destination for many to go home to, to stroll around, to party in, or to show off and to socialize in. But it is also a place to kill for, to become a martyr for, to hide in, to destroy, and to escape from. For an outsider some intimacies of Beirut will always stay hidden, yet its nightlife extravaganza or political violence is very likely to take you by surprise.

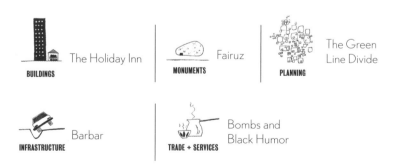

The Holiday Inn

BUILDINGS

Fairuz

MONUMENTS

The Green Line Divide

PLANNING

Barbar

INFRASTRUCTURE

Bombs and Black Humor

TRADE + SERVICES

Photo by Nicolas Bourquin

EMOTIONAL
CITY

Haig Papazian

A WORLD WITHIN A WORLD

As you walk through the streets of Bourj Hammoud, you feel as if you are outside Lebanon, in a different world, even though its limits are situated just a few meters from the eastern perimeter of Beirut, the Beirut River. Bourj Hammoud is a place destined to retain an Armenian identity, and remains culturally distinct from Lebanon. It has been increasingly isolated from its surroundings since its initial construction. This physical isolation has allowed for the suburb to grow into a unique form with a different logic to its surroundings.

Bourj Hammoud is a spatial patchwork of different styles, memories, fantasies, and stories shaped by our Armenian experience. Open space is very scarce – the urban landscape is compact and very tightly integrated amidst the dense urban fabric of buildings occupying most of its spaces. Elements projecting Armenian culture, such as power lines, rooftop and street advertisements and banners, are all part of the vernacular here. To an outsider, there is no line between the mass and the void, and no sense of orientation.

Bourj Hammoud is a made up world at the eastern suburbs of Beirut, with its geographic reference elsewhere, in a place that no longer exists. How can one intervene in such a world? How can it be linked to the outside world and still retain its unique identity?

A FABRICATED WORLD

An outsider's first visit to Bourj Hammoud is a hypersensual experience full of colors, sounds, motion and what seems to be repetition of the same forms all around. It is highly resistant to the process by which a visitor integrates urban space into smaller, comprehensible fragments that enable ease of orientation within different parts of the city. It would be impossible for someone unfamiliar with the area to build

a cognitive map of Bourj Hammoud, because the streets and buildings look so alike at first glance. So many characteristics are repeated; the width of the streets in relation to the height of the buildings, the textures and colors, the power lines dangling five meters above your head. Even an actual map is of little use, because drawings on paper could not convey the spatial experience on the ground.

The first impression someone passing through Bourj Hammoud would get would be of a labyrinth: a dense urban network that never truly reveals itself, and which, once one starts moving through it, has no clear beginning or end. The outsider resorts to creating a reference point to anchor themselves, perhaps an open space amongst the narrow streets, or the municipal square. For the outsider, this point becomes the center of this building/ street/shop/utility/pole/maze. In other words, if you are unfamiliar with these surroundings, you can easily get confused.

For an inhabitant of Bourj Hammoud, the center is nowhere and everywhere. Spaces that seem alike for an outsider are different for an insider and re-present different zones within this fabricated world. Most of these zones are named after different cities in Cilicia from which the Armenians of Bourj Hammoud were deported during the death marches of the Ottoman Turks in 1914 and 1915 (the original cities in Cilicia no longer exist, but their names live on in the different areas of Bourj Hammoud). The different worlds constituting Bourj Hammoud began as unconnected neighborhoods.

These separate little communities grew in an unplanned chaotic way, until meeting at their peripheries to form the current urban fabric of

Bourj Hammoud. Each of these worlds has its own character, with its own church and school. Each is meant to be a self-sufficient community, but the use of similar construction materials, and the use of the same architectural vernacular during the second generation of Bourj Hammoud (from the 1940s to the 1960s), resulted in stylistic uniformity. Industries have merged with dwellings, which have merged with the bazaars, clinics, schools and churches, all within one zone, one world. It is in these worlds that the different subcultures within Cilicia have developed. They exist in harmony within each world and in discord with the other worlds.

A WORLD WITHIN BORDERS

Today, Bourj Hammoud is a world spatially 'estranged' from Beirut. Over the years, different borders have arisen, separating and isolating it from its surroundings. The first of these is the physical barrier that separates Bourj Hammoud from the sea to the north. This barrier consists of a highway for fast-moving traffic that was built in the 1950s to connect the different coastal cities. The highway has become a physical barrier separating these cities from the sea. It is a 30m wide road that cuts through Bourj Hammoud, separating the small neighborhoods that once bordered the sea from those that remain today, and demolishing those in between (Sanjak camp has been cut in two, part of it situated on the southern side of the highway and a small part on the northern side). Large industries proliferated on the northern, coastal, side of the highway, separating it even more from the neighborhoods of Bourj Hammoud.

The second border is a 'gap', situated on the western side of Bourj Hammoud, where a 3m high by 30cm thick concrete wall, constructed in 1968, runs along the Beirut River; this wall creates a physical and visual barrier to the west – Beirut. Before the walls were built people used to cross the river from one world in Bourj Hammoud into other Armenian sub-worlds on the western side of the river – Hayashen (Karm el Zeitoun) and Hadjn (Khalil Badawi). Today, both these regions are known by their Arabic names rather than their Armenian names. Because they are on the western side of the river they are part of Beirut and have therefore become part of the Beiruti, rather than Armenian, culture. The construction of the river wall, followed by construction of two highways on its western side, created a large gap of 90m between Bourj Hammoud and Beirut, and this physical gap has created a social gap.

The third border takes the form of an elevated highway bridge (Yerevan bridge) that cuts through the southern side of the city to connect Ashrafieh to Sin el Fil across the river, the two highways and Bourj Hammoud. The construction of this highway bridge destroyed a line of neighborhoods connecting Cilicia to the Sis and Arakadz regions. Today one can cross under the bridge through a dark, covered area that violently assaults the urban fabric (at places, there is a 50cm gap separating the bridge from some of the buildings). This is not the real edge of Bourj Hammoud, yet the presence of the concrete surface and large pillars of the bridge create a non-physical barrier that – in peoples' minds – separates Bourj Hammoud from Nabaa (Nabaa used to be an Armenian region before most of the Armenians that returned to Soviet Armenia were replaced by Shia from the south). The bridge has become a physical statement separating the Christian Armenian area from the Shia Muslim area; they coexist yet they rarely interact. The bridge did not actually divide, but it gave a reason and a means for division.

The fourth border is different to the other three because it is a human barrier. On the eastern side of Bourj Hammoud, in the regions of Dawra, where a lot of working migrant minority groups from south east Asia and Africa have come to live over the last fifteen years. They form very tight, strong communities at the edge of Bourj Hammoud and they are growing year by year. The resulting barrier is a human one of different races, separating Dawra from Bourj Hammoud. This human barrier has started to filter into the eastern regions of Bourj Hammoud, so in fact it is becoming a mobile barrier, making Bourj Hammoud smaller as it grows.

Within these four different borders, Bourj Hammoud exists with all its complexities and events, which themselves interact with the interfaces that surround it, if only to separate themselves from the others.

A WORLD OF NO LANDMARKS

Because everything is similar Bourj Hammoud is a world with no landmarks. The only buildings that stand out are the churches. They are mostly light pastel colors or white, but the color isn't what makes them stand out – it is their domes. An octagonal dome is found on top of every Armenian church in Bourj Hammoud, although they are out of proportion. What makes these buildings special in this Armenian-fabricated world is what the form and the original function of a church represents for the sustainability of Armenian culture. Can the church still be considered a landmark if it is wholly integrated into the urban fabric?

For outsiders the churches may have become landmarks; a church is the only thing with which they are able to formally associate because it can be distinguished from the rest of the urban fabric.

For an insider though, the place has no significant function as a landmark. For them the churches are merely an expression of their daily life. Every person living in Bourj Hammoud, every character within this fabricated world, has created their own landmarks based on their individual perceptions of this world: a shop, a sign, a wall, a courtyard, a name; the superimposition of all these references within the world makes the world itself a landmark.

A WORLD OF CONSUMPTION AND PRODUCTION

Passing through the wide arteries of Bourj Hammoud that connect the highway to the city, one encounters a new wave of buildings, with the shop fronts and window displays repeating the rhythms one encounters throughout the city. But as you turn into the wide entrance of Master Mall (on the street perpendicular to the Beirut Tripoli highway), you will realize you have entered a ghost town. The mall is uninhabited, abandoned, or rather evacuated, left to disintegrate and stagnate. Originally designed as a place where multiple images of ideal times and places combine to create an illusion of the world or a spatial unity, it has now become a place with no future.

The Master Mall was conceived as a connection between Bourj Hammoud and the rest of the city, through the physical up-grading of the urban environment, consumer attractions, by producing a creative, innovative, exciting and safe place to visit, play and purchase. It was, in fact, designed to replace the Tro Armenian refugee camp. The building that was supposed to facilitate commercial life in fact operated as a blocking mechanism.

The architecture and the spatial aspects of the mall from inside out are alien to the world in which it is nestled. It is better to stay outside and drift through the streets, within the norms of the human scale that one is used to.

Similar buildings with the same purpose suffered a similar fate, going bankrupt and closing down. Only the shops and spaces with façades overlooking the streets were able to stay open, because they continue the city's shopping tradition, a direct relationship between shop and street.

People living inside Bourj Hammoud would rather visit existing shopping strips and markets that line the streets in the different worlds of Bourj Hammoud. Each road being specialized in a certain type of commodity, from clothing to accessories in Arax street, dried fruits and vegetable markets in Marash street, shoemaking in the Cilicia region to jewellry in Armenia Street. All these shopping streets already constitute landmarks for insiders and outsiders, becoming spaces for contemporary flâneurs to shop, meet, and interact in a very active aesthetic of motion, color, light, signage, displays, music – a whole representation of a culture. The Master Mall's inability to replace all these aspects doomed it to failure.

A WORLD OF NO HISTORY AND FROZEN MEMORY
The different early resettlements of Bourj Hammoud were conceived as a physical manifestation of their memories of Cilicia, and so, with whatever material at hand, they created it in the image of Cilicia. But the image itself is an edited version, as Chris Marker said, 'we do not remember. We rewrite memory'.

History and memory have different conceptions of what is past and present. On the one hand history tells of how Bourj Hammoud is constructed, but

memory remembers what it chooses to remember, and that is what lives on. The physical manifestations of tradition and custom in the architecture of Bourj Hammoud are all erased (except in the case of churches) because construction materials, topography, climate and natural resources vary between the homeland and Beirut. What remains is the content that constitutes all the physical manifestations, and the belief that content without form disappears. The content of Armenian culture is based on memory that has been altered and has survived through the events taking place within the different parts of this fabricated world.

In a sense, Bourj Hammoud rewrites its own memory, though based on the collective Armenian memory of the genocide. Bourj Hammoud has become a world that does not relate to anything, neither referencing a place that exists, nor linking with the place it exists within. It has its own hyper reality that allows it to function in its unique way, which allows its inhabitants and visitors to experience its cultural and urban complexity, and recreate their own memories within it, by manifesting them through events that they practice within the spaces of this world, the streets, the market, the school, the churches, the houses, the factories. These events allow for the creation of new memories in this world and enable it to live and survive as an independent entity... not as a world trapped in history.

What could one possibly add to a world like this?

Tony Chakar

IF YOU STOP WALKING NOW, EVERYTHING WILL GO TO WASTE

Fragments from the Catastrophic Space Tour.

Visitors to Beirut often travel solely into the spectacular, the already apparent, the theatrical. Apart from Martyr Square and the Corniche, most of the city's landmarks are places and buildings that refer to war and destruction. The Murr and Holiday Inn towers, the iconic Barakat building, the remnants of the Green Line and the Sabra and Chatilla Memorial Site; many of the first entries penetrate the city from its most vulnerable and its most raw side. But the spectacular is also the obvious, and the obvious isn't very memorable. You'll need photos and cameras to capture it, to remember it.

The following fragments were taken from a beautiful nighttime walk through Ashrafieh, a neighborhood in East Beirut, which was given to us by Tony Chakar, in the fall of 2006. In his tour he proposed, in a way, a number of new entry points into the city. For us, at the time, it was very worthwhile.

The complete tour is available as MP3 on: www.partizanpublik.nl/ catastrophicspace

FRAGMENT 1: SASSINE SQUARE

My tour begins near Sassine Square, which is located on the top of Asrafiyyeh, the hill that gave the local neighborhood its name.

The old city was located between the hills Basta, in the west, and Ashrafieh, in the east. Before it began extending in the nineteenth century, Beirut used to be a very small city. The historical city was located in the downtown area that we know today. It extended from the sea until Sassine Square, and from Martyr Square till Place d'Etoille.

The old streets, that surround Sassine Square, are negotiating with the hill. They always circle around the hill. The new streets however cut trough the old fabric and come perpendicular to the hill.

http://partizanpublik.nl/catastrophicspace/

FRAGMENT 2: IT IS ESSENTIAL TO MOVE

This tour is a result of a container of ideas that I call the Space and Time of Catastrophy. Although the ideas are not very clear yet, they all relate to Beirut and have sprouted from my frequent walks in the city.

During this tour it's essential to move. The idea is that the body is in decay, and everything that it touches is an extension of the body. So what happens when the body meets the extension of the decaying things when the body is already in decay?

It's a very abstract idea, I know. And I don't know where it would lead us but we are here to discover just that, together. Lets go on an adventure. Follow me!

FRAGMENT 3: WALKING IS A SERIES OF CONTROLLED FALLS

I'm, of course, aware of the stereotypes surrounding Beirut. This night's journey is intended however to 'despectacularize' the

image of this city. Let's take it slow, easy going. I know that many of you know this area very well and that there's nothing new that I can show you. I only want you to see it through new eyes. It's always very hard to describe what's in front of you, to find the exact words, but when you do, the whole world is illuminated. It's a beautiful feeling. I will try my very best.

As they say in science: walking is a series of controlled falls. The idea is that you are conscious of this and that you are conscious of the forces of gravity at the same time. We take everything very slowly. We are not marching to conquer anything.

FRAGMENT 4: THE POROUS CITY

There are many unseen barriers in the city. Try to notice them. Each time you make a turn it may become darker, more intimate or visa versa, louder and more public. There is a vague but noticeable hierarchy between streets and neighborhoods. As we're

descending from Ashrafieh Hill, for instance, the streets are becoming more and more private, like small and unique universes that exist in their own temporality.

In earlier times, the passage between the public and the private would be more gradual. The buildings used to have open staircases. People would talk to people outside and in doing so cross the barriers between inside and outside and between the public and the private areas.

Beirut is, or used to be, a very porous city. Everywhere are peepholes to other parts of town. The city always manifests itself in the form of small fragmented images. You can see, or move, between houses and neighborhoods. When the animosity wasn't as large as it is now, this was reflected in the urban make-up of the city. Today, streets and belvederes are cut off for safety reasons. The houses are becoming more and more inwards oriented.

FRAGMENT 5: THE SPACE AND TIME OF CATASTROPHY

As you may have noticed, we just sampled the Space and Time of Catastrophy. We experienced its fragmentation, its different temporalities, and the fact that inside the Space and Time of Catastrophy, everything is an allegory.

I must admit, that for me, everything in Beirut is a metaphor. The meaning of everything does not come from the inside but is illuminated from the outside.

The Space and Time of Catastrophy is a tactile experience. It's the opposite of rational space, where meaning is ordered, understandable and sensible. Inside the Space and Time of Catastrophy you will never find closure, because meaning is never fixed. You can't find a definite understanding either, because reality is fluid. In this realm, things change, shift. Shapes and forms are interchangeable. Everything can mean something else in an eyewink.

FRAGMENT 6: IF YOU STOP WALKING NOW, EVERYTHING WILL GO TO WASTE

One should let the city penetrate oneself through the skin. Experiencing a city is a very tactile experience. It is never a visual experience. If it is just a visual experience it is lost, it is no experi-ence at all. It remains in the realm of the spectacular and the incidental.

When you physically experience a city, going from one fragment to another, your body starts to produce meaning. The city ceases to be a façade. Beauty will stop being an issue anymore. You will experience the fragmentation as nomads, each fragment containing the whole of the universe, and while you are walking from one fragment to another, you take a bit from the place you were to the place you are going to. If you stop walking now, everything will go to waste.

Photo by Nicolas Bourquin

HEAVEN HELL HAMRA
The Civilizing of Appetite

The love trade is a thread woven deeply into Beirut's fabric. It is strengthened by people with a craving for the unexpected, and a spirit of adventure that never dares to seep beyond its original edge. Defining what makes this local business an ongoing success is multifaceted and complex. However, behind each trade lies certain logic. And Beirut has defined the major lines for that logic, however blurry to the oblivious eye.

RED LIGHTS ON THE GREEN LINE

The business of selling sex has been legal in Lebanon since 1931. Lebanese law has allowed brothels to emerge in certain areas, and regulates them under eccentric terms, providing that the women working there are above twenty-one years of age. During the Lebanese Civil War, the area of Zeitouneh located on the Green Line separating East and West Beirut became the hub of the sex trade. Stretching from the east side of the Place des Martyrs (Martyrs' Square) into Gemmayze, area of delineation, named 'behind the bank' served as neutral ground for years of war, allowing the brothel business to remain one of the few unaffected economic aspects of Beirut; fighters from both sides of the Green Line frequented the brothels regularly, as is depicted in Ziad Doueiri's film West Beirut.

After the war, the Green Line no longer existed as a physical space. It physically dissipated along with the sex trade, and nothing remained of either

but for a notorious reputation. The zone was mostly destroyed by Solidere and replaced by the sanitized Siafi Village: up-scale housing replacing budget prostitution. Under the guise of show-dancing, the sex market consequently had to move to what were then the only lively nightspots in Lebanon, namely the three coastal towns north of Beirut: Kaslik, Maameltein and Tabarja. Up to this day, cabarets in those towns employ up to fifteen *artistes*, while some sixty to seventy establishments known as super nightclubs employ as many as thirty girls, mostly from eastern Europe. The girls dance, spend time talking to the customers and encourage them to buy drinks.

With most of the business taking place north of the capital, Beirut, and specifically Hamra, has its own rules for managing 'love'. Obscure bars in Hamra with low-key façades soaking in a red light, cater for wandering lust. With names such as Guy's Bar, Underwater, Goldfinger, Candle Light and Tico Tico, these bars are not places where regular customers come to drink. The entrance is usually guarded by a bouncer and only men are welcome. The doors are slit open and little of the inside can be seen from the street.

LES ARTISTES

Most women catering for eye-candy and pricey evenings are from the former socialist countries, Russia, Romania and Bulgaria, as well as Morocco and Egypt. These foreign women are invited to Lebanon as so-called artistes. Artiste is the preferred nomenclature to describe a nightclub dancer, a masseuse, a model, or a barmaid. But it is also a cover term for the unmentioned profession of a prostitute; the irony is best manifested when these 'non-prostitutes' are required to take monthly medical examinations.

The artistes are brought to Lebanon in groups on a six-month visa. The reason for this tight work period is to prevent actual love or relationships developing with local men: six months is definitely not enough for long-lasting relationships to form, the police are assured. And since these women can only return twelve months after every departure, a ruse is devised to weaken any tie with a local. Some of them, however, revisit sooner using a different passport with a new name: a crack in the system.

102 Artistes are not free to move about alone. The escorts must be escorted. They also have to stay only in hotels approved by the General Security, strictly under the responsibility of the club owner who employs them. He must see to their good conduct. During their stay, the girls will be carefully watched, and police inspectors visit to make sure they are not engaging in prostitution. Ironically, the monthly medical checkups continue to take place.

Beirut has its own rules for managing 'love'

The average daily schedule of an artiste: every night, a mini bus takes the girls from the hotel to the super nightclub around 9:30 pm; their working hours in the cabaret are from 11:00 pm to 5:00 in the morning, after which they are driven back to the hotel. The girls are not allowed to leave the hotel between 5 am and 1 pm, but they are free to go out in the afternoon with the gentlemen who have made appointments with them the night before at the cabaret.

THE ETIQUETTE OF NEGOTIATION

When men walk into bars and super nightclubs looking for some company, they receive it in a rather traditional way. Contrary to what most would think the escorts are not immediately 'at their service'. A ritual has to take place first. The bars and clubs are the intersection between the sacred and the profane. They are at the edge of the city's heart but in the heart of the city. A constant osmosis exists between these places and their context. They feed on the rituals of everyday life to nurture a need in the dark which is not much tolerated in the light. 'Courting a prostitute' is a conflicting expression, yet it describes the way things actually take place in Beirut. Similar to dating, courting is a 'must' before inviting a girl to spend the night. Perhaps this technique adds to the excitement of the meeting. In super nightclubs north of the capital, men splurge on bottles of champagne or liquor before getting a chance to approach any of the women. If they get to sit with a girl, if she buys into the 'courtship', and if she decides to go through with it, the actual

get-together usually takes place the next day. More often than not, such a second day might start off with a small shopping expedition. To advance the courting-game, the man might buy her clothes, accessories, and take her out. Only then may the final act be played out, and the couple meets that same night at a hotel room or a furnished apartment that will turn a blind eye, as they commission a fee for this recurrent service. The men may pay between $50 and $200 for their company and favors, which the girls do not have to disclose to their employer.

HEAVEN, HELL, HAMRA

Rumors abound that next to the artiste scene there is a flourishing call-girl industry, mostly with Lebanese girls, who presumably work in the Gulf and Saudi Arabia. It is said that many college students augment their parents' allowances this way and it is a way for working-class girls to contribute to impossibly meager family budgets.

Finally, there are the much more sinister and decadent activities, which make the super nightclub a sex-trade-lite. The street walkers, African or Sri Lankan, working the highways north of the city who are often in the company of their children. The children appear to be the ones who incite the cars to stop. And there are the homeless boys (Syrian, Palestinian) who solicit on the Corniche.

The dark side of a laissez-faire culture. The sex business in Beirut is a strange element of the city with a dual presence and effect. It is protected by law yet outlawed by society. It marks its existence yet hides its extensions. It organizes entertainment yet entertains disorganization. Some choose to engage in it and others arrogantly ignore it. But very few are ignorant of it.

Beirut, like many other cities is a place where different people live in close proximity, and where civility stands for the rules, norms and values that regulate their lives. With this omnipresent layer of society rubbing against most cultural, religious and social taboos, the sex business provides a rare look into the working of urban civility.

Photo by Nicolas Bourquin

HAMRA'S IMAGINARY GRAFFITI

Jounblat, Souarti, Emile Eddé, John Kennedy, Mansour Jurdak, Mohamed Abd El Wahab, Omar Ben Abd El Aziz. These are a few of the streets named after families or personages.

We were walking in Hamra, discovering new territory, taking every unfamiliar turn, trying to map the area. Two old men running a barbershop couldn't resist the urge to inquire, seeing two young girls with a bunch of papers and pens, a camera, and hungry eyes. They called the street Sitt Nassab, I imagined Sitt Nassab as a typical Lebanese housewife with a broom in hand shouting at kids on the street. I tuned back to reality for a moment to find out Sitt Nassab was the mother of Fakhreddine (a Lebanese prince from the early modern period).

'Sourati family is living in the building over here, and Maamari family used to occupy the whole of Maamari Street, then they lived over there, now a parking space, and this famous writer Constantine Zuraik, Allah rest his soul, they named the street after him, and...' That's all I managed to hear from the man with the mustache before imagining how all these people would react if they were to come to life today. Some proud to have a street named after their family, some disappointed seeing what had become of their street, their homes, and their culture. Sitt Nassab staring in disbelief, trying to make something out of the completely alien sur-roundings, memories of her life provide a little security, an old familiar tree brings back feelings of nostalgia; and a few cats here and there.

TEENAGE LOVE

For International College (IC) students, the first make-out place is always the amphitheatre - 'the love stairs'. As teenagers, we could still be fooled into giving it the reverence that befits places so ancient as amphitheatres - in fact the structure was modern enough to be made out of some sort of cement. In any case, it faced the sea, and acted as a stage where the sunset was the daily show. It had an aura, if only for the innumerable first kisses, first cigarettes and other 'first times' it witnessed.

But make-out space is also class-conditional. Those teenagers whose parents could not afford IC also found themselves a spot, which was majestic for being ancient - except theirs was genuinely ancient. They went to the roman baths behind Banks Avenue near Riad-el-Solh, and below the Serail. The dig was on a landslide, at an angle, and so the archaeologists built a small makeshift staircase over it, and little flights of stairs running up and down were connected to each other with little wooden hanging bridges. Here and there they built small wooden 'rafts', overlooking the whole site. The bit of greenery and the ancient stone, in the proper spotlights, made for dream material.

Yet another choice nearby was the backyard of Al-Omari Mosque downtown, just across the street from Karam restaurant. This was another spot forgotten by the Adab police, where the lighting made for a less theatrical but cozier mood.

Then of course, the big advantage of Beirut is its sea front. Couples used to stray away from the group and sit on the rocks below the little light house, near the lower cafeteria that had the best burgers ever sold on the beach. (I've never climbed the lighthouse, but to set the mood, my boyfriend climbed it and described to me from up there a breathtaking view, and it can't have been completely made-up).

It takes creativity for young lovers to find their place in Beirut.

We used to eat on the beach, watching the fishermen. By night, the fishermen went out in large groups, each carrying a little lamp on his boat, to attract the fish. From the shore, they looked like constellations on the black surface of the sea. I would make a bet that many more boys and girls watched them, from other, less enclosed areas along the coast of Beirut - from Ramlet el Bayda, from the little hills rolling down towards the sea once you jump off the fence of the Corniche, and from the covert corner behind the big cement block at the base of the large post on AUB beach. The Druze of Jal-el-Bahr also jumped the feeble fence of the old fishing port, crouched by the sea roughly facing

Riviera Hotel, and barely visible to the main road.

Where else? The stairs of Gemmayze leading up to 7ay el Saras2a and its beautiful houses, and the staircases off Rue (not Avenue) Charles Helou. For the francophones among us surely the CCF and its beautiful garden.
And as far as they count, Farayya motels when we

Couples used to stray away from the group and sit on the rocks below the little lighthouse, near the lower cafeteria that had the best burgers ever sold on a beach.

---

were old enough to drive, the only inconvenience being that we always went up in groups to make it look like a skiing trip, and it was always awkward to make out in one room knowing that two other couples of your friends are doing it in the adjacent rooms – it's just not meant to be a group endeavor like that. Yet the evenings spent having wine and roasting marrons in the fireplace were worth it.

One trick was to park the car just anywhere and cover it with a hood.
I was very impressed with my boyfriend when he did it, only to find out the third time around that the Adab police were onto this a long time ago. They waited till we started the car to go home, drove right next to us and banged on his window asking him to stop. They wanted our papers, but my boyfriend played it cool enough, and I made enough drama, for them to let us go –'for this time'.

SUSPICION

Why are you here?
Seriously, there
must be something.
Something fishy.

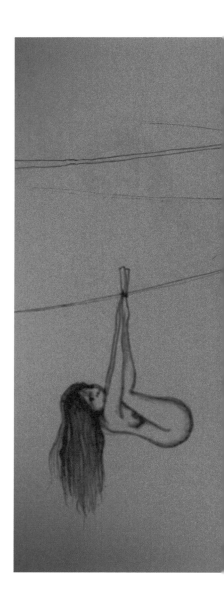

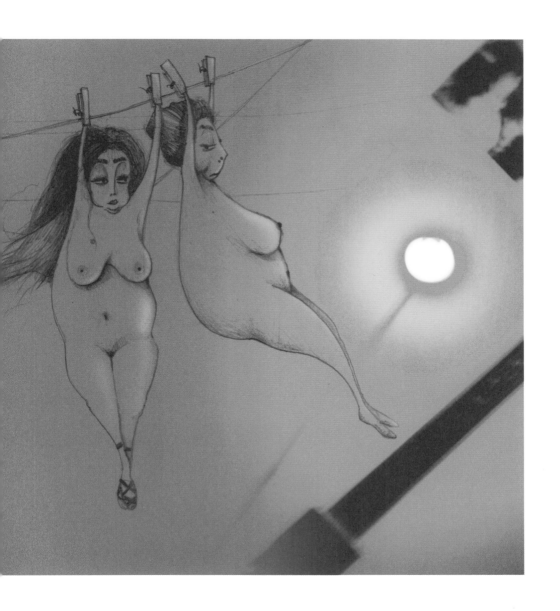

From little kids to old people, they want to know who you are, where you are from, why you are here, and, if the purpose of your visit is credible, what exactly do you think about them, are you with them or against them, who is your enemy, there must be something, how did you get here, why, why the sudden interest in our area, you look strange, are you telling the truth, do you believe in God, do you believe in my God, there must be something.

BLACK MARKET

With Hezbollah having a strong influence on some of the piers in the Beirut port, Dahiya has products on offer you will find nowhere else in Beirut (apart for the kitschy yellow Hezbollah accessories), making it the biggest smuggled-goods market in Lebanon. Crappy Chinese kitchen utensils, cigarettes from Syria or Iran, bootlegged copies of the latest movies... Anyone?

GAY AT SASSINE SQUARE

Two boys, naked on the central Sassine Square. Castigated, humiliated, disrobed and dumped by the police. Caught while kissing in an alley. Homosexuality remains a complex issue in Beirut. Open affection is a very tricky pastime. A kiss might be paid off painfully.

Sexual conduct against the laws of nature is punishable by the maximum of one year in prison, dictates Article 534 of the Lebanese Criminal Code. Although open to many interpretations, the article covers homosexuality according to Lebanese courts. Likewise, criminalization of homosexuals is backed up by the greater part of society. Few gays and lesbians will overtly admit to it when bluntly asked. Most of them lead double lives, at least for their families. They justly fear expulsion or sometimes even honor killing.

Yet, the situation is more nuanced in practice. 'Coming out' doesn't always turn out miserably, the elite vanguard of Beirut openly accepts homosexuality. The first Arab gay organization, 'Helem' (acronym of Lebanese Protection for Lesbians, Gays, Bisexuals and Transgenders) was founded in Beirut in 2004. The organization fights for equal rights and wider understanding. Its website offers a forum,

psychological assistance, information, and supportive 'coming out' stories.

Homosexuality has obviously made its modest entrance in society. Public condemnation is not an option any more. Progressive Beiruti strongly disapproved the incident on Sassine Square. As an explanation for the rise of liberal influence, most people point to Beirut's exceptionally diverse character at political, cultural and religious levels. Another reason is found in its position at the crossroads of western and oriental civilizations. Yet, in some way, westernization paradoxically thwarted daily life for gays. While two friends walking hand in hand is an innocent habit in many Arab countries, it will actually cause aversion in Beirut's urban culture.

Despite prevailing intolerance, today gays, lesbians and bisexuals can quite easily find their way in Beirut's incontestably energetic underground scene. Even though all barkeepers claim to be straight, the city offers a huge quantity of popular gay or gay-friendly meeting points. Gay nightlife ranges from snug taverns, dimly lit nightclubs, funky discos and lesbian karaoke bars, to exuberant thematic parties at altering locations. It is here where Shia Hezbollah's, Sunnis, Maronites, and other religious and ethnic minorities gather in relative discretion to meet, talk, dance, laugh and sing. Homosexuals from the entire Middle East come to Beirut's scene to escape their own countries' more severe regimes.

Underground at night, gay life is booming, but by day in public space, it hardly seems to exist. Yet, as you wander through the streets of Beirut, and pass by a DVD store, it is not exceptional to find a copy of 'Milk' in the display window, winking at San Francisco of the 1970s.

Lebanon Out of The Closet
A short film on Beirut's gay subculture produced by Dateline, a program on Australia's SBS TV. The piece also features an interview with Helem member Ghassan Makarem
http://news.sbs.com.au/dateline/lebanon_out_of_the_closet_130488

Lebanese group wants ban on homosexuality lifted. Hurriyyat Khassa seeks to abolish law which stipulates one-year jail sentence for sexual intercourse against nature.
http://www.middle-east-online.com/english/features/?id=11610

Helem, http://helem.net

DEAR MOM, DO YOU GET IT NOW ?

Do you know
How I feel once I walk in the door
Knowing that I'll see you there
And the lie will start to begin
Another time, again and again

...

I want no more fighting
I need no more discussions
I can't handle everything by myself
'cause we all need help
But not in the way you do it

...

I'm just so stressed because of it
I don't wanna talk about it
I'm very sick about it
Don't wanna look on it

Just tell me why
Is it too hard to accept it
Eighteen years finally I admit it
6,000 days, I finally accept it

I'm not ashamed about it
Very proud about it
So much happy with it
I think you can understand it

But I guess God was wrong
If you're the one who's right
I'm sick, I can't come and go
I don't wanna see my face
I need to change this place
Going somewhere, just not here

...

I just want you to move on... now
I'm gonna do the same
But I need your support
And try to understand now
Good things go without coming back
And time cannot be rewind

Hichou, posted on the Helem website,
Saturday, July 28, 2007. Fragments

THE UNDERTAKER OF EAST BEIRUT

Possible only in a land of protracted conflict, Joane Chaker shares stories of an unlikely man, basking in mythical celebrity.

He has become an urban myth. Not all the stories we tell about him can be assigned to any one undertaker with certainty. Like a brand that becomes so popular that its name comes to stand for the product itself, this character has come to stand for all undertakers in East Beirut

His little lugubrious store stands in the narrow back streets of Ashrafieh, where a person not born in the area would rarely set foot. Some of the merchandise is displayed outside against the wall in the shade of an alley – three or four coffin lids, of different sorts of wood and various designs.

He is a notorious 'brand', and a rich man. After all, his business does well in times of peace, and it does better in times of war, poverty and famine. Also his clients are never in the mood to bargain for a better price.

Until the reestablishment of some form of state in the 1990s, he drove around in a large black American car, with tinted windows and an accompaniment of motorcycles. When it parked, a man stepped out from the back seat, a black suede cowboy hat covering long gelled-back hair, shades, dressed in black from top to toe and the shirt open well down to the middle, to show off abundant thick, black chest hair and many heavy gold chains of various sizes, and many large rings on his fingers. He would show up like that to the funeral of his more socially prominent clients, walk in as if walking into a restaurant, and sit down with the family of the deceased to write the Na'we paper (a small flyer of a standard format that is posted in the streets to announce a person's death, and the time and place of the funeral). And he would be

painfully casual and business-minded about it... 'eh (yeah)...so do you want to write it down like this?... is it alright like that? I have to get going...'

The fact that he was the sole supplier of the militias of East Beirut during the war, made this undertaker so famous.

For those deaths, he had ready-made templates of the Na'we paper, as speed was important in these cases for reasons of political propaganda. The party often wanted to make the most of the funeral procession and to do it within the hours that followed, as it was great advertising. The long procession parading the coffin through the neighborhood was a sign of the power the party enjoyed in the area. As soon as he got the phone call: 'quickly, we need you to spin something up, make it good...' The undertaker's first question would be, where was he killed? And the answer determined the Na'we template he would use. If the young man was killed in Ras el Nabe' or Shiyeh, it was surely in a battle against the Palestinians. Then he used the template, which stated: 'He fought and died a martyr in the name of Lebanon.' If, however, the young man was killed in Jounieh or Karantina, he used the template which read: 'He fought and persisted, and was killed by unknown cowardly fire,' as that was probably a battle between Christian factions. Speed was so essential that sometimes the undertaker was contacted while the young man who got shot was still alive and bleeding. And it seems that there were incidents were the young fighter finally survived. And then the issue arose of the very strict 'non-exchangeable, non-refundable merchandise' policy. 'It will not go to waste, you will surely need it one day,' was his argument...

Photo by Nicolas Bourquin

FLOUR FACTORY

Photos by Tarek Moukaddem

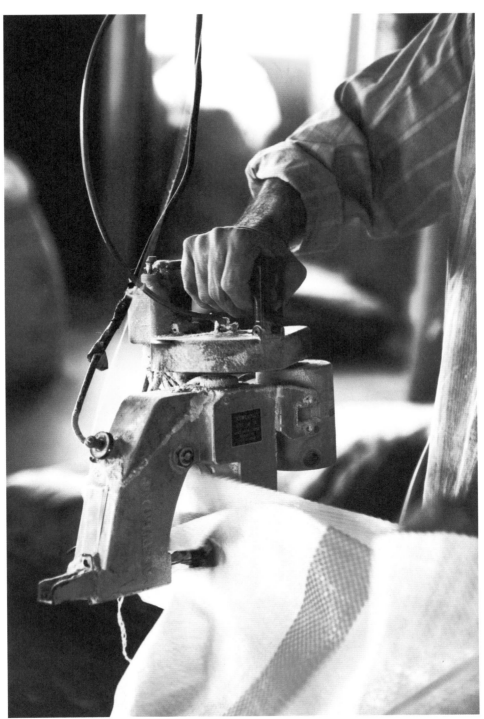

A TOWN OF THEIR OWN

'The form of the city changes
much faster than the hearts
of the humans.'

Jacques Roubaud

Taking advantage of sketchy legal frameworks and governments too weak to enforce rules and regulations, the hardworking Bourj-Hamoudians have taken the issue of housing shortage in their own hands. They started building new dwellings from scratch and adapting existing junk for their own purpose, like the missing Middle East Airline stands glued to a small house under the bridge.
I was never taught armenology but visiting Bourj Hamoud was somehow very familiar and strangely disquieting...a town of their own.

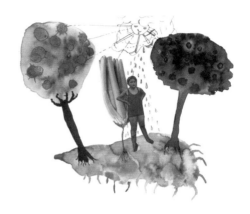

In their own town, Armenians can shop and work tranquilly in their native language. They want to see their kids and their neighbor's kids succeed, and they don't want to loose their culture.

Exploring Bourj Hammoud never gets boring. Getting lost in the narrow alleys of this insular community is a feast to the senses. The feeling of swimming in a flood of colorful cells, electrical cables forming floating veins massively intertwined, connecting inexplicably. I swam in a corny ocean of signs and shapes, small details filled with laughter... and tears...laughing tears...hysterical laughs...emotions wildly overlapping. These emotions where little by little shaping reality, emotions prompted by necessity, laughter being a possible form of communication.

Ara, twenty-three years old, born in Bourj Hammoud, opened up about his city: 'It is very conservative. It's not the right place to find a bar or a nightclub where youngsters can mingle. As a reaction, the youth now carries images of physical decay and the infestations of social vices.' The Young people of Bourj Hammoud, the modern creatures of the after life, mostly hang out in the Shopping Mall. Most specifically the internet café. Many people say we live both a physical and a virtual life, and these two realities are getting more intertwined every day.

As I continue walking through these narrow streets, it hits me. Something is happening that is not happening. These streets I'm stepping on are only for walking through, not for staying in. A city evolves over time, through history and war, but to what extent can we develop this boundlessness between our ego and the outside world? As I was turning back to withdraw from the 'modern city', I was trying to pick up some glimpses of public space along the way, collecting some fragments of possibility... And suddenly sparkles of relief came along as I stopped and looked closer at the markets. All these artisans, businessmen and craftmen were injecting new energies to make the barriers disappear, and keep the conversation going. These markets are little heartbeats interacting between each other, creating opportunities of exchange of information, debate, decision-making and deliberation between the inhabitants. Self made men, they were. At that moment, misery and neglect didn't matter anymore, this love for life was contagious. The sun was still shining, filling the atmosphere with a warm joyful vibe. I continue my festive walk with this never-ending thirst for another intriguing vision.

BURJ HAMOUD IS
GONE TO HEAVEN

FISH MARKET

Photos by Tarek Moukaddem

Inventing urban stories and identities is a technique frequently used in city branding campaigns or the entertainment industry. Beirut consists of a multitude of stories and with just as many heroes, all campaigning to dominate the view on history. As elsewhere, urban culture in Beirut is produced bottom-up as well as top-down, from outside and from within. Through the enormous quantity of new construction activity, and the variety of intervention to existing conditions, a visitor can recognize a certain restlessness to reconstruct, to renew, or to realign the present in reference to a certain past. A cocktail of nostalgia for an earlier past, trauma of the Civil War and the dream of a comfortable home produce high and low culture, night and day life, and public and private spaces.

Beautifully Decorated Modernist Mayhem

BUILDINGS

The Singing Statue for Rafik Hariri

MONUMENTS

The Valet Parking

PLANNING

Use the Arab GPS - Ask How to Get Somewhere a Few Times Along the Way

INFRASTRUCTURE

Accept Chewing Gum for Change

TRADE + SERVICES

INVENTED
CITY

Michael Stanton

MODERNISMS

Documenting the modern architecture of Hamra, where
the art of the period of independence meets contemporary
minimalisms (to be continued...)

On a side street in Ein el Mreisse, next to the mosque, sits the doomed residential building designed by the Polish architect Karol Schayer and his partners. It is a slab that was sandwiched between the narrow street and the sea before the Corniche was extending in the 1970s across the front of houses, fishing harbor, mosque and this modern masterpiece. The southern street façade is arranged in vertical panels, modulating stacks of horizontal windows with a monumental stair held behind a grid of tilting windows. At the eastern end trellises shade large windows facing public rooms. The northern seaside façade is arcaded, holding terraces facing the sea, a repetitive frame attached to the building. Jean Marie Cook, who lived and taught in Beirut before, during and after the Civil War, lived in this building and recalls many parties where she and her guests would descend from her terrace to the rocks in front of the building and dive into the Mediterranean.

The building has recently been stripped of all metals and hardware, the intricate railings and delicate window frames torn out in preparation for what seems inevitable demolition. The neighborhood is a frenzy of new construction, vulgar towers with vast apartments rising where vernacular houses or cool modern structures had recently stood.

The Gefinor complex up the hill from Ein el Mreisse represents a high-water-mark of late Modernist urban *sange-froid*. Curtain-wall slabs hover over a travertine plaza designed by Victor Gruen and his associates. A public street cuts through the complex, a groove in its icy surface. The sensual curves of a hanging spiral stair contrast in verse to the elegant geometric prose of the project.

On Souraty Street, just to the west of Abdul Azziz, towers the abstract slab designed by Joseph Philippe Karam. Again its abandoned and stripped character implies that it may soon be destroyed although its height of thirteen stories may save it, or at least offer its skeleton for some tawdry make-over. A play of square one-floor high panels alternating with voids defines the southern façade and casts necessary shadow in this too-light-rich climate. This simple motif is extraordinarily powerful, a minimalist expression covalent with contemporary experiments in the arts, of the sublime geometries of Alice Neel or Donald Judd, of the same period.

The block to the east of Abdul Azziz on the south side of Hamra Street was the first planned modern development in the area. On the eastern end is the Horseshoe building by Schayer and partners, the first all glass curtain wall office structure built in the region and named for the famous café that occupied its ground floor and contributed to the dynamic street culture of an international and libertine Hamra before the Civil War. Next to it to the west is the Hamra building with one of the seventeen underground movie theaters that also galvanized activity on this teeming promenade. The Hamra, designed by George Reyes, contrasts to the Mies van der Rohe glazed clarity of the Horseshoe with an equally rational façade composed of stucco panels and steel frame windows in a binary and elegant pattern that recalls the pre-World War Two work of Le Corbusier and other modernist pioneers. On the western end of the block a tower was intended, marking the kardo and decumanes that Hamra and Abdul Azziz formed in Ras Beirut, the site of two more lost cafes, Modca and Wimpy diagonally across the intersection. Wimpy was famous for its original Eero Saarinen's tulip chairs, two of which were kept for private viewing by the owner after the 1980s for it was here that two Irsreali officers were shot dead, kicking off a punishing resistance to their occupation. The metropolitan legend is that their blood still stained Saarinen's design icons. Both cafés have closed recently, replaced by low-end international clothing chains, reflecting the demographic and commercial adjustments this turbid neighborhood has undergone.

In the Hamra building is the last of the old haunts, the Café de Paris. Its quirky deck chairs and lights remind of a more idiosyncratic if not bohemian period here. The design of the block included an inner-block street leading to the Alhamra bowling alley and on to the area now made into a continuous festival by the Barbar empire of food shops, a gastronomic souk of exceptional quality. In this area are a series of architectural splendors. The power station, one half block to the east on Edde Street by Schayer presents a De Stijl composition of panels and lines to the street, sadly damaged by the opening of an enormous door in the façade simply to install a new generator, desecrating an important building and demonstrating the almost total lack of regard for the really superb quality of the works of the '50s, '60s and early '70s. Vernacular stone and colonial French recreations tend to define what quality is here, identifying a universal Mediterranean standard that is becoming generic, from Southern California to South Korea. It is indeed true that this sort of architecture has a heritage in Lebanon, and is charming in its simplicity and repetition, but its recreation is usually tacky and suffers from the worst aspects of pastiche. On the other hand, the great modern architecture of the city and nation both recognized the environmental conditions that sponsored more traditional forms and the quiet directness those forms present. Yet, these traditional forms are not cheap imitation, a fault even the French recreations in the downtown - so lovingly restored - are guilty of.

Vulgar towers with vast apartments rising where vernacular houses or cool modern structures had recently stood.

Up Edde Street, past the weird but ebullient Royal Garden Hotel with its hanging foliage making an almost green building long before this was a fashion, is another of the exceptionally brilliant Joseph Philippe Karam's designs, an apartment block with particularly developed response to its location and characteristics. On the side street the building steps back in a series of stacked masses defining each floor. These give way to a repetitive series of balconies on the main street, each forming an L, punctuated by screens that recall the mashrabiya grills of the region. Around the corner, on Rue Jean D'arc is another of Karam's residential projects, a play of shifting panels with a screens shielding the main staircase...

At this point in the tour of Hamra everything changes for, as I was photographing the last building, I was accosted by a man on a motorscooter who tried to pull my camera away from me. Only after a scuffle did he identify himself as a security officer, demanding to know why I was taking pictures and who I was. His colleague, so high on drugs he could not stop talking and shaking, said they were from the FBI. The situation was dangerous and abusive, given that I could have escalated into real violence since it appeared I was being robbed. In fact, it turned out, after he took my camera and more officers showed up, that they were part of the contingent of semi-official police patrolling the area around the Hariri compound, several blocks away. The sentence should read: I was taken to their station and interrogated, photographed, my local contact details established, and then I was allowed to leave but forbidden to take any more pictures anywhere near their zone of influence. Thus, again, the political realities of a traumatized nation intervened to contradict the aesthetic values that nation once espoused, and should still! The qualities of Karam's Astra hotel around the corner by the Commodore Hotel or of Alvar Aalto's project on Hamra, for instance, or of Khalil Khoury's Sanyiah Garden building or Interdesign structure, will have to be discovered, and documented covertly in this paranoid present.

Photo by Jeannette Gaussi

WALKING TOUR WITH HASSAN CHOUBASSI

01. START: LOUNGE DE PRAGUE

We meet thirty nine year old artist Hassan Choubassi in Café de Prague, a favorite meeting place in Hamra for the cultural scene of Beirut. Although Choubassi is a visual artist and scenic designer who teaches at the Lebanese International University (LIU), he prefers to tell people, when asked, that he works as a postman.

On this sunny February afternoon in 2009, Choubassi is going to take me for a walk. I'll find out that he knows every stone and notices the smallest changes. He shows me his Hamra.

Choubassi lived in Hamra for over twenty years. Since he moved to East Beirut in 2003, he is still in Hamra almost every day, to meet friends, have a coffee and to walk around.

Choubassi explains: 'My uncle lived in Hamra in an apartment in Karakas at the end of Hamra Street. He left it when he had to escape during the Israeli invasion in June 1982. He had a job offer in Iraq, that was a safe place back then.'

'After the evacuation of the Palestinian militants from Beirut (from 21 August until 5 September), the Lebanese army entered Beirut. My father felt then that it would be safer to be in Beirut and we moved into my uncle's apartment. My father was wrong. Only a few days later, on 15 September, the Israeli invaded the city. I was only twelve years old, but I remember every detail of those days.'

'When I was nineteen years old, in 1989, I went to live by myself in the same building in another apartment on the tenth floor. My uncle had already been back in his apartment on the ninth floor since 1983.'
– We turn right, right and walk to the center of Hamra.

02. CENTER OF HAMRA

The center of Hamra is where Wimpy and Modca used to be. These cafés are gone but most people will still know where they were.

'My parents owned an apartment in East Beirut, but it was occupied by Christian militias, the Lebanese forces, during the war (since 1976). In 2003 my family got the apartment back and now I'm living again in this apartment where I was born. This is why I left Hamra. Although it is almost six years ago, I still don't feel at home in East Beirut. That's why I've

never really left Hamra. However, after 7 May 2008 I don't go as much to Hamra as I used to do. To explain this I have to go back to one of the events of the Civil War that took place right here in the center of Hamra.'
'In 1982 two Israeli soldiers were killed at Wimpy Café by a member of the Syrian Social Nationalist Party (now an ally of Hezbollah), called Khaled Alwan. The square is named after him. Now and then there is a fight over this street sign between the Syrian Social Nationalist Party and the Future Movement or Hariri Movement. Since 7 May 2008 you'll see two young men protecting this sign, thus showing that their nationalist party is now controlling this street. Since May 'they' are more present, you can feel 'them' and you'll see small clashes. They want to show they took control over West Beirut, that they're controlling this region. They've taken the city hostage.'
'Nobody can claim Hamra, as many different sects are living here. That's why it suffered a lot during the war. Many clashes took place in the center of Hamra. One of the heaviest battles was in 1984 or 1985 when, after the withdrawal of the Israelis, the Cowboy (the militia leader of the Druze or Progressive Socialist Party) fought against Abou Khashbeh, also known as The Father of the Wood (now head of security for the President of Parliament, Nabih Berri). Also in the period between 1986 and 1988 a lot of similar small wars took place in Hamra.'
– We go left and walk to Costa (on your right).

03. COSTA

Costa used to be Horse Shoe Café – a famous café for the Arab intellectuals. Here you would find those intellectual Arabs who had fled to Lebanon to escape their dictators. Horse Shoe was closed in the early eighties and was transformed into one of the first fast food restaurants of Lebanon. Hamra, one of the cultural centers of Beirut, has a special history when it comes to nightlife. It's notorious for it.

04. CATHOLIC CHURCH

Have a look at the Catholic Church on your right.
Because Hamra is mixed, you'll find mosques and churches in this area. The first inhabitants of Hamra were the Sunni and Orthodox Christians. Later the Druze and Maronites and Roman Catholics came. The Shia came in great numbers after the Israeli invasion in South Lebanon in 1978.
– We continue to Medina Theatre (on your left).

05. MEDINA THEATRE

The Medina Theater used to be Saroula Cinema, it was closed at the end of the war. Most of the changes you see in Hamra involve the disappearance of places that have a history.

06. MONTREAL CINEMA

Montreal Cinema (on your right) is open and shows Arabic movies. For English movies you should go to Concorde, Empire Ashrafieh, Starco, Sodeco Square or one of the many other cinemas around the city.
Theaters in Hamra also feature companies from abroad.

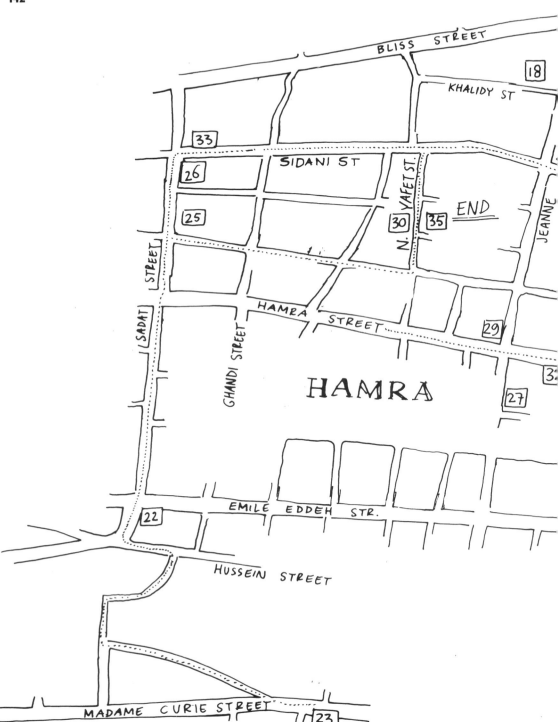

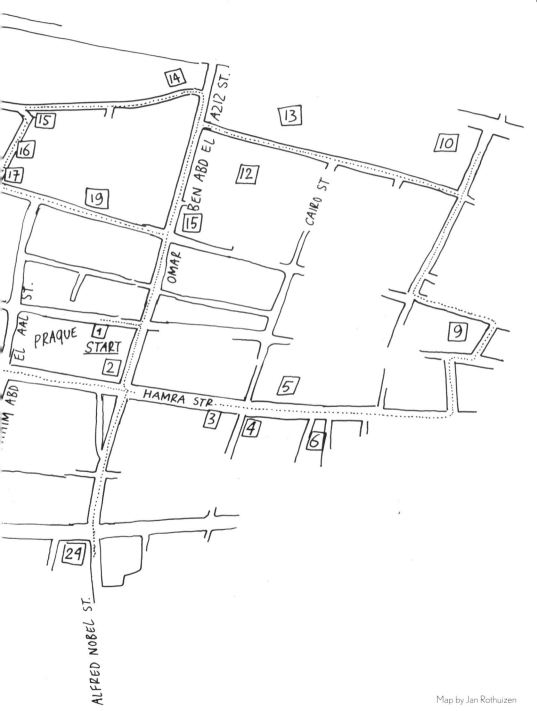

Map by Jan Rothuizen

07. MINISTRY OF TOURISM

See the Ministry of Tourism at the beginning of Hamra Street.
– We go left.

08. NATIONAL BANK

The National Bank (you see it in front of you) is at the beginning (if you go in the same direction as the traffic) of Hamra and is a symbol for the commercial function of Hamra.
In the late 1950s Hamra became the commercial center of Beirut. The American Trans-Arabian Pipeline Company settled here near the Hamra cinema. They actually built an oil pipeline from Saudi Arabia to Tripoli, although it was never used. The Domtex building was built to house the foreign employers who came mostly from the US. Much of the architecture of Hamra Street dates from that period.
The Syrian-Lebanese Commercial Bank (you'll find it opposite to Domtex) is the first modern building. It was built as the office building for the pipeline company. Shia refugees from the South occupied it during the Civil War. The building has been empty since 1995. The inhabitants were evacuated after the liberation of the South and went back to their villages.

09. MARONITE CHURCH

See the Maronite church on you left. You can see the Aresco Palace from here. It's the only steel building in Lebanon.
'The different groups that live in Hamra don't mix but co-exist, usually peacefully. Because Hamra is more mixed, people are not hostile to one another. You could say that Hamra is the most public neighborhood of Beirut. You can drink in the street where you will also see veiled women. In Dahiya for example, drinking in public places is forbidden. And in East Beirut you won't see many veiled women.'
– We turn left and left again.

10. GEFINOR BUILDING

See the Gefinor building on your right, a commercial center since the 1960s.

11. NEGATIVE BUILDING

Look for the 'negative building', an open white square behind the building.
'I like to walk here. It's urban and empty at the same time. You can see the sky from here. It's the only place in Hamra where you find nothing. It is surrounded by buildings; you would almost feel there is a building missing. That's why I call it the "negative building".'
This place is known for its many travel agencies, now also restaurants are opening here.
– We turn left and left again and walk through the American University Hospital.

12. AMERICAN UNIVERSITY HOSPITAL

See the American University Hospital.
'Hamra has existed for more than a century. The architecture tells of the evolution of the area and life in Hamra. The current borders of Hamra run from AUB to Hariri Palace and from the beginning to the end of

Hamra Street. The relation to AUB is paradoxical as the AUB is Hamra's "raison d'être" but also blocks it from the sea.'
Before the late 1950s the buildings were limited to residences around the AUB. The AUB started in the late nineteenth century as a protestant missionary center. That's when Hamra was first inhabited, before you would find only lemon trees and cactuses in Hamra. Some streets are named after the Sunni and Christian families who owned the land back then.
– We go right.
'If you look left, you can see a street that passes underneath a building. It reminds me of a street in Amsterdam. I studied there for a couple of months and continued my habit of walking around. When walking in Amsterdam I always missed Beirut, so I gave the streets the names of their "Beiruti twins".'

13. ISSAM FARESS HALL

See the Auditorium, the Issam Faress Hall (part of AUH) for cultural events and conferences.
– Turn right.

14. BAROMETRE

See Barometre, a small dive where one loses track of life, on your left.
We read graffiti on the wall, it says (in Arabic): 'The Orient God's heaven is Beirut'. We don't understand what it means.
– If you went left you would find the best manouche (rolled sandwich with cheese) place.
– We go left and take the quietest street of Beirut, Makhoul.
'I would love to live here. This street has also a "twin street" in Amsterdam, a street that has the same silence.'
See the Evangelist church and the Orthodox church.

15. BLUE NOTES

See Blue Notes, a famous jazz club in Beirut.
We go left and take a small quiet street.

16. FIRST HOUSES OF HAMRA

Look at one of the first houses of Hamra.

17. CONSTRUCTION SPACE

See the construction space – here there used to be a very characteristic hybrid building that was built in the 1940s and reconstructed in the 1970s.
We go right, and right again, to Flying Pizza.

18. FLYING PIZZA

'Flying Pizza is a place from my youth. Beirut is not so big, but it is complex and intense – that makes you nostalgic. Although it was a difficult time back then, I enjoy the memories I have. I go over them again and again. I think about the good things, like flirting with a nice girl in my university freshman year. Memories can heal you.

19. LE ROUGE/WALIMAH

'We pass Le Rouge. Check this street, a whole new environment is building up here with new bars, restaurants etc. Check also Walimah restaurant further in the same street, a good place for Lebanese home cooking.

20. LEBANESE AMERICAN UNIVERSITY

The Lebanese American University (LAU) started in 1924 as a college for women. As it was the only university in the Middle East that would accept women, all the princesses of the Middle East studied here. The LAU has one of the biggest libraries in Lebanon.
- We go left and left again and see the barricades that are there to protect Hariri's son; since 7 May 2008 there are more roadblocks. Hamra has some famous inhabitants, not only politicians like Hariri and Jumblatt are living here. One of Jumblatt's neighbors is a famous pop star called George Wassouf (who is said not only to be very famous but also to be famous for being very macho).

21. CITY CAFE

The former owner of Horse Shoe started City Café. The somewhat older, rich intellectuals come here. 'My father always goes here, not that he's rich.'

22. COLLEGE PROTESTANT

See the College Protestant
- We pass City Café again and pass Royal Garden Hotel.

23. ROYAL GARDEN HOTEL

Also see the special about the Royal Garden Hotel in this guide.
- We go left and are back at the center of Hamra.
Hamra Street is a shopping street but now many bars and clubs are also opening here. These moved out of the center of Beirut after it was occupied in 2006 by Hezbollah supporters for a protest against the government. First Monot and Gemmayze became trendy and now Hamra is upcoming with new sushi bars and design bars. Especially on the weekend, traffic fills the street until 3 am.
We're going to Bliss Street.
- We go left, left again and left again, and then we go right and right again.
We're getting a bit tired. Choubassi is testing whether I've lost my sense of direction - if I had one - and indeed I am getting confused. I start asking Choubassi for his favorite places.

24. AND 25. BISSAN BOOKSTORE

'Check Bissan Bookstore (25) a good Arabic bookstore, check Ristretto (26) for a nice breakfast.'
- We go right.

26. RISTRETO AND 27. YOUNIS CAFÉ

'For breakfast you should go to Ristretto (26) or to De Prague for a good omelette or croissant. You'll find the best coffee in Younis Café (27).'

28. REGUSTO AND 29. NAPOLITANA

'For lunch or dinner you can choose from Regusto (28), Pasta di Casa (not on the map) and Napolitana (29).'

30. NAPOLEON, EMBASSY

Sleeping: Napoleon, Embassy (for I've heard it's cheap but ok).

31. ANTOINE LIBRARI AND 32 CHICCO

Buy yourself a good book at Antoine Librairie (31) or a DVD at Chicco (32).

33. LIQUOR STORE

There is a very small, but good liquor store where young people go to buy their own drinks.
We pass de Prague again.
'Recently the Syrian embassy has opened in Hamra. It is emotional and difficult for me to have a Syrian embassy here because of the traumatic relationship between Lebanon and Syria. Of course it is an important statement to show that Lebanon is an independent country that has diplomatic relations with Syria.'

34. MAYFLOWER HOTEL

Choubassi drops me off at the Mayflower Hotel where I'm staying, four hours after we met. I wonder how it is possible that we walked and drove for such a long time in a relatively small area. Then Choubassi gives away his secret and explains about the meaning of walking:
'I'm walking in overlapped circles to keep on walking in the same area. I walk between coffee and whiskey. I walk alone, with my girlfriend or with my best friend Tony Chakar, I walk with whoever is ready to walk. I'm a city watcher. The walking is about surveillance, seeing people and criticizing. While walking it's like I'm guarding, controlling, preserving Hamra. I'm constantly making comments inside, nagging "why did they do this, what happened here?" And sometimes I see nice things, like nice graffiti. I always wish I could bring good things I see elsewhere to Beirut. I wish I could change something, something that would make it easier to live here.'

Illustration by Hanane Kaï

Alex Nysten

150

FROM RAOUCHE WITH LOVE

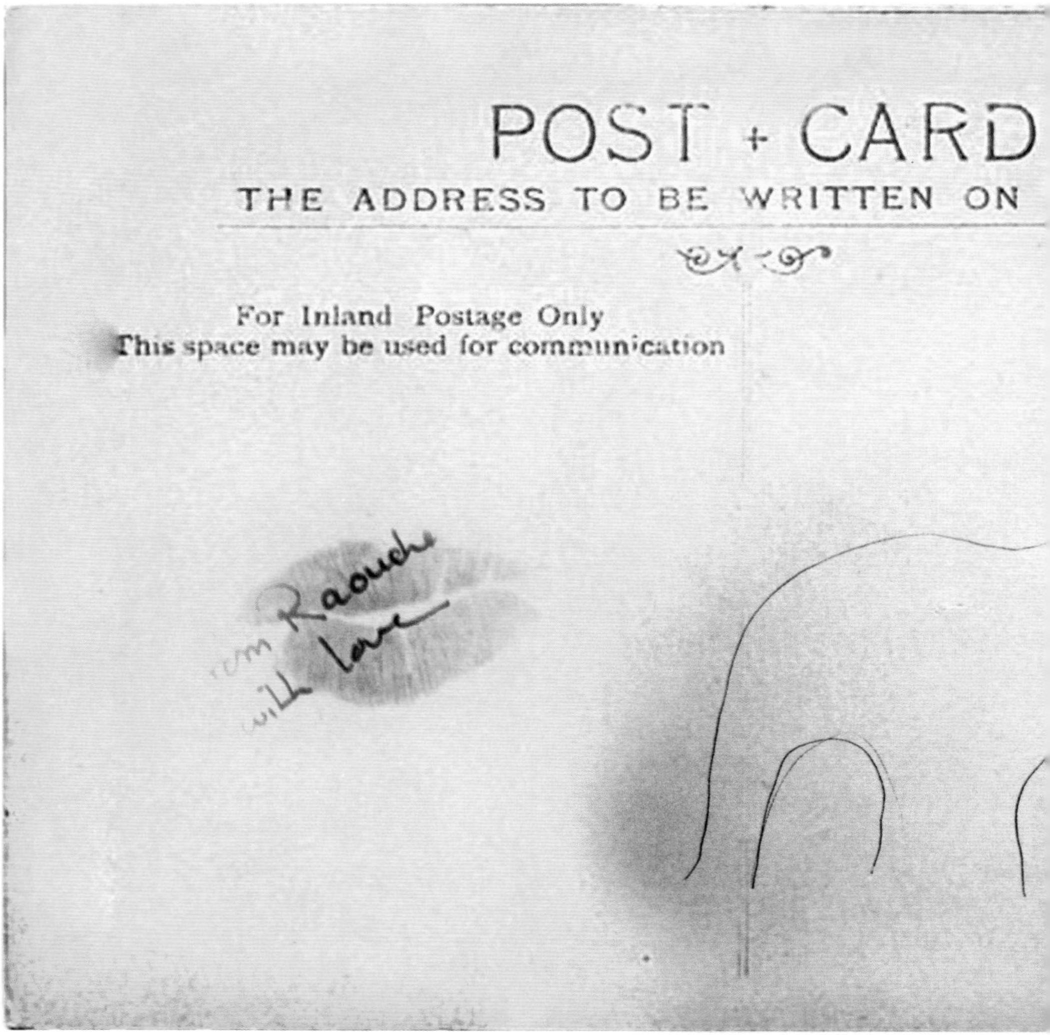

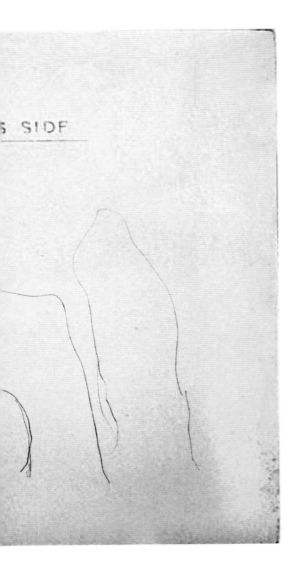

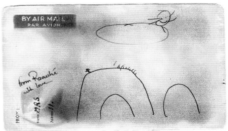

MENTAL MAPS

In many bookstores and newspaper stands on Hamra Street you can buy a wide range of maps of Beruit. On most maps however, the larger part of Dahiya is either cut off or covered by advertisements. This bustling and crowded part of the city seems to be intentionally neglected; at the Tourist Information Office they will tell you: 'There is nothing to see there. It's not a good place, why don't you go visit the beautiful cedars in the north?'

Random people on the streets were asked to draw a 'mental map' off the top of their heads, showing the main roads, the places they frequently visit and how they perceive the other - often despised - surrounding parts of the city.

A friendly manager of a kitchen store draws Dahiya as the pumping heart of Beirut with the main roads as arteries. The owner of the Buns & Guns restaurant says: 'If you want to get a beer, you should go to the Christian part', while he is drawing a small bottle on the map. A simple street plan is drawn reluctantly by a hasty passer-by. A group of kids with school bags are commenting fanatically on the comprehensive map that one of them is drawing: 'If you want to eat, you should go here under the bridge where you can buy the best belila or here you can smoke the narguile.' Without hesitation they draw the Hezbollah convention center: 'Here the main Hezbollah events take place. When Nasrallah gives a speech they show it on a big screen.' When their maps reaches the outskirts their faces change: This place here is very poor, it's a Palestinian area. 'We don't like those neighborhoods in the north; I have lived there, there is no freedom; you cannot breathe', one of the boys exclaims. 'Neighbors complained all the time when we were playing in the house. Here we solve our problems amongst each other, without police interference. If we can't solve a problem ourselves we'll ask either Hezbollah or Amal for advice.'

1. Tripoli
2. Beirut
3. The Dahiya
4. The Airport
5. Tyre

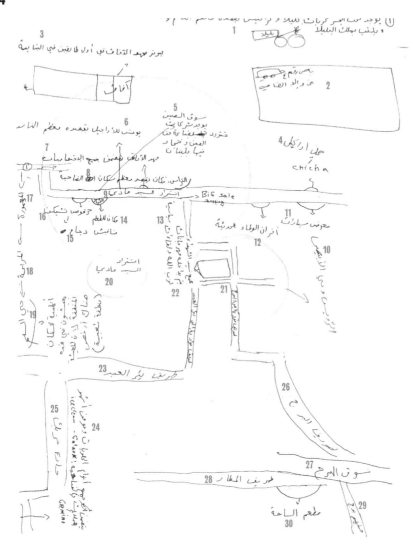

1. Under the bridge, there are carts, one of them sells the best belila, they call him the 'king of belila'
2. To get to or from the Dahiya area, take bus no. 4
3. The first two floors of the building
4. Waterpipe store
5. Chinese market with companies that import their stuff from China
6. Most people go to this place, it's the best waterpipe store
7. A real small college with the most majors
8. On the first floor opposite the big market there is a good coffee place. Most people from the Dahiya come here
9. Street named after the son of Hassan Nasrallah

10. Orweiss and Hay el Abyad
11. Car showroom
12. Main bakery in town
13. Hezbollah convention center where main events and speeches take place, mainly through satelite television
14. Al Khabez, place to eat
15. Chicken Manoushe
16. Harkous Chicken
17. Ma'amura
18. Maraijeh
19. Hai-Sillom. Most people live in this area, because it's the cheapest area in town
20. Estrad Sayed Hadi
21. Road to Bourj
22. Road to Bir el Abid
23. Bir el Abid

24. Store called Gremino. He sells gateaux and ice cream. It's the most famous store for sweets in Dahiya
25. Haret Hreik
26. Road to Bourj
27. Bourj Market
28. Airport Road
29. Palestinian camp in Bourj al Baraizne
30. Saha restaurant

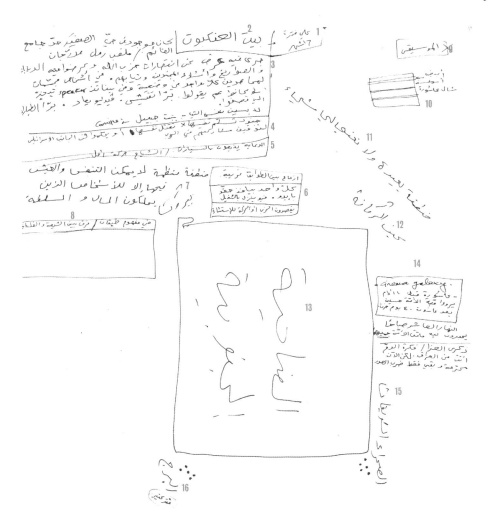

1. Duration of six months
2. Spider House
3. It used to be in the Sfeir area, next to the Al Kaem Mosque. On a two level sand field they showed the victories of Hezbollah over Israel. They displayed captured tanks, missiles, helmets and other weapons of Israeli soldiers. There were statues of fighting soldiers, loud speakers, smoke, video's about the fighting and loud sounds of airplane bombings. The fighters were dressed in the same military clothes as when they were fighting in Beit Jbeil
4. The people of Solidere either surrender, kill themselves or talk to the Israelis to stop the involvement in the war
5. Loudspeakers in car / Chiah Amal party
6. When there is unrest or disturbance between two floors, everybody takes the law into his own hands. For example, you are allowed to hit your employees. When things get out of hand, they go to Amal or Hezbollah for mediation
7. A very organized area of Beirut, you can not breathe there. Living there is only for people with a lot of money and high ranking government positions.
8. The difference between Shia and Palestinians, social level
9. Music

10. White and Black Achura scarf
11. A far area, that doesn't mean a thing to me
12. Ein el Remmeneh
13. South Dahiya
14. Cinema Galaxy. Here they celebrate
15. Achura for ten days. They tell the story of Imam Hussein. Forty days after Achura is a very sad day.
On the tenth day of mourning, they killed Imam Hussein: the whole nation died. During Achura there is mourning and people hit themselves, until they bleed. The ritual came from Iraq, but now it's taboo and people kept the tradition of hitting their hand on their chest
16. Shwayfet Desert
17. Bourj, very poor

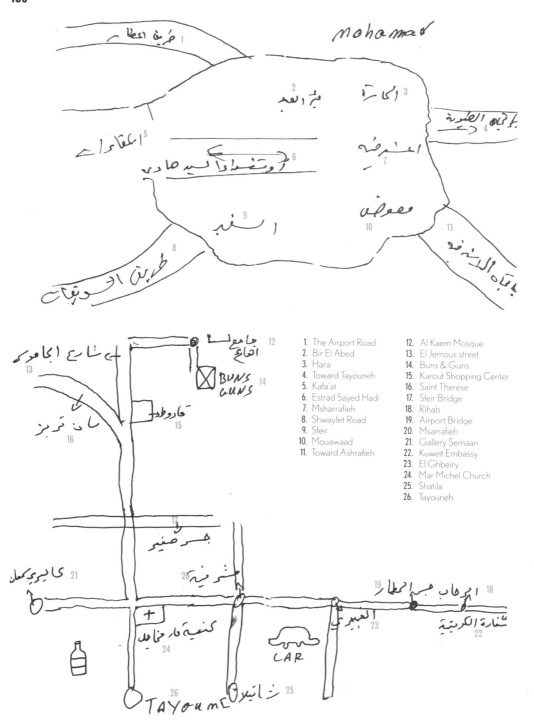

1. The Airport Road
2. Bir El Abed
3. Hara
4. Toward Tayouneh
5. Kafa'at
6. Estrad Sayed Hadi
7. Msharrafieh
8. Shwayfet Road
9. Sfeir
10. Mouawaad
11. Toward Ashrafieh
12. Al Kaem Mosque
13. El Jemous street
14. Buns & Guns
15. Karout Shopping Center
16. Saint Therese
17. Sfeir Bridge
18. Rihab
19. Airport Bridge
20. Msarrafieh
21. Gallery Semaan
22. Kuweit Embassy
23. El Ghbeiry
24. Mar Michel Church
25. Shatila
26. Tayouneh

FLIPPER BALL

Be prepared for a hectic adventure of mixed emotions...

Inside Dahiya, you are a shiny pinball that stands out in the crowded space. Be prepared for a hectic adventure of mixed emotions. It's actually very simple: you just have to stay inside and beware of the hole.

You get tossed and flipped to many places and faces. You have only three chances. I believe we lost two chances in the end. But it is absolutely worth the try.

1. Ain Al Remmene is one of the areas surrounding Dahiya. Residents of Dahiya don't visit this area much because of political differences ●
2. Do you need a makeover? Whether you're a male or female, you can always visit Centre Lorence in Shiyah for a new hairstyle ● **3.** The Nike Outlet shop in Siyyad sells Nike shoes remaining from previous collections ● **4.** Cinema Galaxy is the last cinema remaining in Dahiya. One of the cinemas that were closed, Cinema Palace, was turned into a motorcycle shop ● **5.** Al Shoueifet is one of the areas surrounding Dahiya. It can almost be called a desert ● **6.** Hungry for alcohol? You can find what you're looking for here in Al Hadath ● **7.** Stories and Impressions about Dahiya ● **8.** Al Tayoone Region ● **9.** Hay Al Amerken means the American Neighborhood in Arabic. It was given this name because of its very calm and organized atmosphere. So you can imagine the stereotype some people have for American life ● **10.** Buns & Guns; faster than a bullet; is a restaurant in Dahiya with a complete military set, from decoration to menu items ● **11.** Pictures of Martyrs you will find everywhere you turn ● **12.** Karout, or in other words, Wonderland; the market for all your desires! Bowls, socks, toolkits, old, new, circles, squares... It is located in Jamoos Street ● **13.** Vietnam is a Paint Ball location for those of you who want to experience getting shot :) ●
14. Malek Al Balila i.e. The King of Balila, is a very popular man who sells a variety of traditional Lebanese food in a wagon. It is located under the bridge at the end of Al Sayyed Hadi highway ● **15.** Beit Al Aankabout i.e. the spider's house is where the victories of Hezbollah during the war of July 2006 were projected ● **16.** Al Ka'em Mosque ● **17.** Hay Al Sellom Region ● **18.** House of Donuts for extra sugar and caffeine :) ●
19. Refresh is a café that was mainly used as a meeting point for 'love birds' :) It was closed one year later...no one knows why ● **20.** Do you think you can have China in Dahiya? Visit Souk Al Seen and be amazed with all the Chinese products you will find! ● **21.** The Adidas Outlet shop on Al Sayyed Hadi highway sells Adidas shoes remaining from previous collections ● **22.** Café Ahla Aalam i.e the Best People, challenges your techniques of card-play. You can find most of the youth hanging out there ● **23.** Fern Al Wafa' bakery Load yourself with mixtures of Lebanese starch experiments ● **24.** Car Expo. If your feet are in pain, pick them a nice car to complete the tour ● **25.** Msharrafiye Region
● **26.** Har'oos Chicken is the zoo of chicken sandwiches ● **27.** Cocktail Al Rida isolates you on an island of fruit drinks and cocktails ●
28. Big Sale clothes shop is the new definition of cheap ● **29.** Istirahat Al Naoora is the last cafe remaining for your romantic expeditions ● **30.** All the DVDs that you can find! ● **31.** Chi Cha restaurant is the right place to go to if you like floating in Nargileh smoke clouds ● **32.** Haret Hreik Region ●
33. Al Khabbaz i.e the baker, makes clones of the traditional Lebanese Mankousheh ● **34.** Cremino is a place for the sweet lovers.You will find a wide variety of sweets, and people in there. It is located in Haret Hreik ● **35.** No Photographing; You need authorization to explore your artistic flushes in photography. If you don't have authorization, expect to be captured and questioned for several hours like my friends, from the workshop, were ●
36. Beirut is one of the areas surrounding Dahiya. Residents of Dahiya don't visit this area much because they think people there are boring and too organized ● **37.** Ahhhhhhhhhhhhhhhhhhhhhhhhhhhhhhhhhh!! ...Scream your head off in Sweet Land amusement park ●
38. These three bumpers are the main headquarters of Hezbollah; Malaab Al Ray, Moujammaa Sayyed Al Shouhada', and the once Mourabbaa Al amni that was destroyed during the war of July 2006 in Lebanon. All festivals and religious rituals take place here ● **39.** Al Rasool Al 'Aatham Mosque and Hospital ● **40.** Shhhhhhhhhhht! ● **41.** Al Borj is one of the areas surrounding Dahiya. Here you will find the Palestinian refugee camp ● **42.** Who are you? What are you doing here? Who are your friends? Why should we give you a chance to stay in Dahiya?... Security Flippers decide whether you can stay in the game or you will be kicked out ●
43. Golden Palace Dress Code: Wedding outfits, Event: Wedding in Dahiya, Bar Code: MMM | FFF ● **44.** Motel, Museum, Restaurant Al Saha is the only place in Dahiya where you can rest your eyes. It includes a museum about the traditions of the Lebanese village, a library for Hezbollah publications, and a restaurant to fill your tummies ● **45.** If you are an alcoholic, please proceed to the next city :) ● **46.** Mahattet Al 'Aytem Fuel Station. The money gained from this station goes to the orphaned children ● **47.** Thank you for visiting Dahiya :) ● **48.** Please enter two 500ll coins to begin the DAHIYA FLIPPER GAME ! You will be transported from Hamra to Dahiya in bus no.4

AN UNEXPECTED HISTORY LESSON

Less than a century ago a lot of mimosa trees, wild strawberries and raspberries used to grow in this area. It used to be agricultural land. Very low yield. There were some small estates but they cultivated crops for domestic use only. Most of the area was wild.

The woman from the municipality forgot all about our request for a permit - something that would allow us to roam the streets, take pictures and ask weird and unsettling questions - and was frantically sketching historical layers on a photocopied cadastral map of the Armenian neighborhood.
'Look, the land was owned by a small number of Maronite families, of which the Khouri family, the Chikhang family, the Sabbagha family and the Kahwaji family were the most notable. Here, here and... here!' With a blue ballpoint she circled the areas where, according to her, the old estates used to be. 'The mansions and the houses for the workers were the only stone buildings standing in what is now called the municipality of Bourj Hammoud.'
We listened quietly, only asking questions when she seemed to pause, keen on her to elaborate as much as possible. Beirut is a city where history is a very, very political topic and where a common interpretation of history is very, very scarce. The National Museum, for instance, only exhibits artifacts from prehistoric times to the medieval Mamluk period. After the Middle Ages, national history seems to stop. Popular wisdom holds that the different denominations in Lebanon disagree on the facts, and how to interpret them. So, in a city where there is no common historical narrative, unexpected oral histories are just as legitimate as any other.

We were sitting in a small office in a municipality building on Armenia Street, a small space crammed with paper files. Our host, an enthusiastic civil servant, who was in charge of the cadastre, among other things, was sitting behind her desk, hardly visible, hidden behind mountains of paper files that were spread over her desktop. Later we discovered that she was even sitting on some. She turned out to be an excellent storyteller, casually dispatching subordinates to search for old photos or cadastral maps to illustrate her history.
'The Armenian refugees first settled in Karantina, on the opposite bank of the river, where they were living in slum-like conditions. The owner of the area, someone who wasn't happy with their presence, regularly set fire to their wooden ad-hoc dwellings. Circumstances were bad. Every day the priests were burying somebody. After a particularly destructive fire, the notables of the Armenian community decided to take action. Their eyes fell on the land on the opposed bank of the river. They negotiated a good price with the Christian landowners and bought the land with their own money. After they settled, the Armenian families in their constituencies slowly reimbursed them.'
From the start the Armenian congregations grouped together around five urban cores, which were called Marache, centered around the Church

of the fourteen Martyrs; Sis, centered around the Church of Sourp Sarkis; Guiligia, who shared their Church of Asdvadzadzin with the congregation from Adania, and Sanjak, centered around the Church of Sourp Vartan. With red pencil she now marked the location of the churches and circled the areas where the old urban cores used to be. 'The names of the neighborhoods reflected the geographical origins of their inhabitants.'

After a small pause in which she stared at the map, she smiled and pointed to patterns in the urban grid, which suggested some sort of planned urban development. 'Although they came from humble origins they were quite rational in their approach to the new situation. In a bold move the notables asked or hired an urban planner to draft a city plan for them. The outcome was a dense and rigid urban fabric that corresponded to their needs. The houses were grouped close together to address safety concerns and each neighborhood was built around a church and a community school. Although the urban planner outlined the general framework, the neighborhoods themselves grew in a very organic manner. The churches were wooden constructions at first, but once enough money had been collected, stone ones were built. The individual houses were erected in somewhat the same practical manner. First people would build one

room, then another, after which they would start a craft or a small factory in the first room, earned some money and began building a new addition to the house, etc., etc.'

The administrator now pointed to the coastal area, north of the coastal highway. 'This was still undeveloped land and because most of the Bourj Hammoud area was still uncultivated they didn't conceive any public areas. The river and the sea were close. They picnicked on the beaches and on the riverbanks. Until the 1950s the sea area, the strip of land from the autoroute to the shoreline, was still in its natural state. From the '50s onwards this area was developed as an industrial zone. Some of the richer Armenian merchants, mostly those in the leather industry, also put up shop there.'

She highlighted a plot close to the autoroute. 'In 1939 another party of deportees from Sanjak came to Bourj Hammoud. Sanjak used to be part of the French Mandate but the French secretly agreed to give the area to the Turks. The story goes that on one particular morning the Armenians discovered that the French garrison had left during the night. Afraid of what the Turks might do to them, they decided to flee and take refuge with their relatives in Bourj Hammoud. They built what is now known as Camp Sanjak.'

Camp Sanjak was a slum area behind the municipality building. When we strolled through the camp after our meeting, we discovered that the municipality had demolished a big part of it and was in the process of expropriating the rest. From the residents we learned that they're developing a big real estate project with a lot of parking areas and that some, not all, of the occupants got a small amount of money and dispersed to other areas in Bourj Hammoud.

Bourj Hammoud is still predominantly an Armenian neighborhood, but it is becoming more and more diverse.
'Between 1940 and 1947, Maronites and Shia came to live in Bourj Hammoud. After 1946, when Soviet Armenia opened its borders to accept members of the Armenian Diaspora, some Armenians in Bourj Hammoud accepted the offer and left for Armenia. Some of the houses that were left behind were

bought by shia refugees from the south, people who had fled their homes during the war with Israel. The Maronites came from the mountains to Adana and the limits of Dora. They settled between and on the borders of the Armenian urban cores, and alongside the river in the Mar Doumet area. They also build Mar Youssouf, the church in the center of Bourj Hammoud.' She circled the areas where the Maronites settled on the map and highlighted the location of Mar Youssouf.
After she was finished and after we downloaded her collection of old pictures of Bourj Hammoud taken, according to her, by the Chikhang family when Bourj Hammoud consisted still largely of uncultivated lands, we obtained our permit. We never used it. In contrast with other neighborhoods at that time, there were almost no security forces present in Bourj Hammoud. We walked, talked and we took pictures without ever being asked for our ID, our permit, or our intentions.

Photos by permission of the Municipality of Bourj Hammoud

THE FREE REPUBLIC OF BOUNYAKISTAN

Attention all Bounyaks and Bounyaquettes!

'Guides are pretty dull' she said whilst gently bending her head, causing her long tousled raven locks to get stuck to the trunk of one of those palm insects they call a tree. 'I'm fed up with my every-day routine and I'm looking for a sharper approach.'

'We don't need another guide. We don't need another Prophet. We need an army.' While drawing hard on yet another half-smoked cigarette, she uttered: 'Let us build up a religion, let us build up a new high temple, the new Jerusalem or let us nuke it all. In fact, have your guide, but let it serve as a rally-ing call. Let it be shocking and un-common. Let's do it. Seems al-ready appealingly outrageous.'

'Like the Royal Navy needed Jack Sparrow, like the United States of America needs Homer Simpson, like Barbapapa needs Barbabob, like the galaxy needs Zaphod Beeblebrox, Beirut silently craves for the Bounyaks. The new pillars of our faith, the chosen Freemen

who will lead us to our freedom beyond our glass coffin.'
Bene Gesserit was the ultimate false Prophet, for it is not fear that is the mind killer, but boredom. And following the never-aging fa-mous words of our beloved idol Jarjar Binks 'errrr, ummmm, blips, welll, ahhmmm, her, heeere wee goh...' we are reaching beyond the skyline of any known Prophets; we are reaching for the profits.

Some say we should scorch the skies, flip every single rock in this city and shave our women bald to redeem ourselves. We will have none of that. We will unleash the Bounyak in each and every one of us, have him roam our souls and tickle our spines. For all of you who are fed up with read-ing and are still patiently waiting for sense in this heap of letters we say: 'Wait!' Serendipity is all about looking for a needle in a haystack and finding the farmer's daughter.

For all of your sinners out there: heed this call. You don't need to

stick your head in stockings to be a pundit. You think Cinderel-la really enjoyed it? You think Al-ice did the rabbit? You think a cat can wear leather boots on a hot tin roof?

Prepare to be shocked and awed. If Tinkerbell could break the code, I am sure you can.

COMMUNIQUÉ NUMBER ONE OF THE PEOPLE'S LIBERATION FRONT OF BOUNYAKISTAN

Fellow Bounyaks and Bounya-quettes, following a series of ter-rible incidents where individuals have preposterously misused the Bounyak identity in order to get some public and media attention, we, the Members and the Head of the Executive Tactical and Strategic High Committee of the People's Liberation Front of Boun-yakistan (the 'M.H.E.T.S.H.C.P.L.F.'), have decided in our blissful wis-dom to issue this communiqué in order to clear up the definitive and irrevocable conditions that define a Bounyak.

Illustration by Pascale Harès

Let it be known as of today that a Bounyak or a Bounyaquette is:

- One who roams a desert or any sandy surface looking for stray undomesticated camels or dromedaries.
- One who is mocked by camels or dromedaries for pursuing them in a desert or any other sandy surface for the purpose of domesticating them.
- One who is mocked by a camel or a dromedary or any other creature for having a genetic and ancestral fear of dogs.
- One who is chronically late for no reason.
- One who drives, smokes, drinks, uses the mobile phone, turns up the music volume and complains of the bad driving conditions in synchronization.
- One who is repeatedly denied entrance visas to any part of the known world, including great parts of Bounyakistan.
- One who preposterously uses the word 'preposterous'.
- Most residents of the secret capital city of Bounyakabad.
- Any non-Bounyak adopting a Bounyak way of life.
- One who uses seriousness as a plan B (i.e. when every other irrational method fails).
- One who exports Bounyak traditions into other societies thus converting them to Bounyakism.
- One who can add even more preposterous items to this shortlist.

By the powers invested in us, the M.H.E.T.S.H.C.P.L.F. solemnly declare these guidelines are, from now on the cornerstone of the Bounyak identity and its new path toward reaching its preposterously outrageous past glory.

May all Bounyaks and Bounyaquettes live freely and preposterously.

May the Almighty Supreme Bounyak preserve your shades.

EXPRESS
yourself

(FOLLOW YOUR NOSE)

Once a place of exchange of aromatic ingredients, traditions, recipes and tastes, Beirut's central souk has now been traded for a fancy, clean and chic city center. The downtown now lacks its authentic tastes and smells. Yet the city retains its flavor in many places, locations only discoverable by following your nose!

Beirut's position along the sea, around a safe and secure bay, made it 'food' rich through trade with the outside world. The arrival of the Armenian people in the early twentieth century brought the textures and smells of mante, sou borek, mohamara and lahm b'ajin. Street food is a staple in a city like Beirut, once found in its old souks it can be a quick snack, a sophisticated sweet or savory food that is often difficult to prepare at home. A sunset stroll on the Corniche will lead you to all you might wish for. Termos (lupine), Boiled Corn, Kaak (bread) to begin. The aroma, the noise and sights all coming from kitsch-adorned rolling carts. A shawarma at Bouboufe (charcoal grilled), a crunchy falafel (the best are at Sahyoun on Damascus Road), or a very Sunni Beiruti foul (at Sousseh in mar Elias) are some of Beirut's best street food 'expressions'.

Around the corner, but definitely not a street food, is Ashghalouna, where food is served in the wonderful garden every Friday at noon. It is the best Sunni Beirut home food experience, à *ne pas rater*! Beirut is also home to Bouzet Hanna, in Mar Meter area. Hanna remains in one of the last crumbling buildings. He is the old man who never smiles, but still produces yummy ice cream, filled with pistachio, rose, lemon or apricot that tastes and smells of the East. For a sweet tooth, kenefeh provides a typical breakfast. Beirut had great Arab pas-

try makers, and Bohsali still makes delicious knefeh every morning sweetened, baked, smooth cheese in bread. Yet the best (in my opinion) are not in Bourj Hammoud but at Ichkanian in Zokak el Blat, which has been in business for some sixty years, and still making the thinnest lahm b'ajin ever.

Food and culinary traditions are expressions of who we are, where we live, our history and the stories we carry. In my opinion (again), a city should be expressed through taste, before sight or sound! Here, Beirut expresses itself well.

Maureen Abi Ghanem is an architect and a lover of all cities. • Romy Assouad is a freelance animator and web designer. • Hisham Awad is a visual arts graduate, and writes about film, architecture, and their mutations. • Cleo Campert is a professional photographer since 1988, wandering artist since 2000. • Joane Chaker is unemployed and so checks her mail once a month. • Tony Chakar is an architect and writer. He teaches at the Academie Libanaise des Beaux-Arts (ALBA), Beirut. • Zinab Chahine graduated in graphic design and designs jewelry. • Steve Eid is a landscape architect and full time cab driver. • Christian Ernsten is partner in Partizan Publik and editor at *Volume* Magazine. • Christiaan Fruneaux is working on some highly secretive writing projects. He lived and worked in Jakarta, Damascus, and Beirut. • Edwin Gardner is theorizing his way out of architecture, only to end up in the middle of it again. • David Habchy is a professional vegetable consumer, he illustrates and animates when he's not eating. • Mona Harb is associate professor of urban planning and policy at the American University of Beirut. • Pascale Harès is a graphic designer and a design teacher. • Jasper Harlaar is a nurse without borders, a student in medical anthropology and sociology and an allround traveler. • Janneke Hulshof likes people, but became an architect. • Hanane Kaï is a graphic designer who likes to illustrate and take photos. Karen Klink is a young Lebanese illustrator currently living and working in Barcelona. Her latest works are site specific art and children's book illustrations. • Niels Lestrade says 'somewhere I got lost in notre dame Beirut, her Saint Chapelles, her Boulevards, her Centre Pompidou...' • Mona Merhi is a writer for theater, radio and television and is currently working on a children's book. • Elias Moubarak is a documentary director, and a photographer. • Tarek Moukaddem is still looking for what he is. • Kamal Mouzawak is the founder of Souk el Tayeb, he is also a food and travel writer and a board member of the Slow Food Foundation for Biodiversity. • Joe Mounzer is a Lebanese architect still living in Beirut. • Alex Nysten is a Finnish-Lebanese masters student in digital animation at Pratt institute NYC. • Nienke Nauta is the founder of Pearl Foundation, supporting Lebanese initiatives for cultural and social projects. • Ahmad Osman is a graphic designer. • Haig Papazian is an architect, video artist and violinist in the Lebanese group Mashrou' Leila. • Pieter Paul Pothoven is a visual artist. • Rani al Rajji and Joost Janmaat are currently establishing Lebanon's first hostel in Gemayzeh and a moonshine bar in Amsterdam; making it real easy for everyone else in this colophon (and beyond) to live happily ever after. • Jan Rothuizen is an artist who lives and works in reasonable happiness. • Ruben Schrameijer is a rambling street psychologist and fictional rock star! • Reem Saouma is a landscape architect. • Michael Stanton is an architect, teacher and writer living in Beirut. • George Zouein has a love and hate relationship with the modern world, living between the edges of reality and imagination.

Initiated by Studio Beirut
Supported by Partizan Publik, Archis, Pearl Foundation
Second edition, printed in Beirut, April 2010

Editorial team
Rani al Rajji, Joe Mounzer, Steve Eid, Christiaan Fruneaux, Joost Janmaat

Chief Editor
Christian Ernsten

Art directon
Jeanno Gaussi, Nicolas Bourquin

Design
Pascale Harès, Jeanno Gaussi, Nicolas Bourquin

Cover image
Jan Rothuizen

Distribution
Idea Books, www.ideabooks.nl

Copy editors
Wendy van Os-Thompson, Steve Rushton, Jonathan Hanahan, Amelia McPhee

Publisher
Archis, www.archis.org

Printer
Al Hurriya, Beirut

Copyrights
Stichting Archis and the contributors

ISBN
9789077966549

ARCHIS **partizan publik** studiO

PEARL

Prince Claus Fund
Netherlands Embassy in Lebanon
Fund Working on the Quality of Living
Beirut World Book Capital

 Koninkrijk der Nederlanden

 C
Fonds
Prince Claus Fund for
Culture and Development

Stichting Fonds
Werken aan Wonen

 بيروت عاصمة عالمية للكتاب **Beirut World Book Capital**

In collaboration with the Ministry of Culture

Special thanks to
Hiam Bachir Saouma, Ole Bouman, Lilet Breddels, Tony Chakar,
Edwin Gardner, Cara Khatib, Bernard Mallat, Caro Mendez Nelson,
Arjen Oosterman, Jan Rothuizen and Michael Stanton.

The collaboration, which led to *Beyroutes*, started with Archis RSVP # 10
Unbuilt Beirut in November 2006. Archis RSVP Events are tactical
interventions initiated all over the world. They are response-based events of
which the content and format is determined by input from their participants.

Interested? Email Archis at rsvp@archis.org